Northborough

in the

CIVIL WAR

Northborough

in the

CIVIL WAR

CITIZEN SOLDIERING AND SACRIFICE

ROBERT P. ELLIS

Charleston   London

History
PRESS

Published by The History Press
Charleston, SC 29403
www.historypress.net

Cover image: On this float in Northborough's 1916 celebration are Civil War veterans George Allen, John F. Johnson, Henry Burdett, Hazon Leighton, William Bemis, Cyrus Mentzer, Orin Bailey, Daniel Sawyer, William H. Warren, John Hart, Levi Whitcomb and Guilford Heath. The "Goddess of Liberty" is Heath's daughter, Annie.

First published 2007

Manufactured in the United Kingdom

ISBN 978.1.59629.220.8

Library of Congress Cataloging-in-Publication Data

Ellis, Robert P. (Robert Patrick), 1935-
    Northborough in the Civil War : citizen soldiering and sacrifice / Robert P. Ellis.
       p. cm.
    Includes bibliographical references.
    ISBN 978-1-59629-220-8 (alk. paper)
1. Northborough (Mass.)--History--19th century. 2. Northborough (Mass.)--History, Military--19th century. 3. Northborough (Mass.)--Social conditions--19th century. 4. Antislavery movements--Massachusetts--Northborough--History--19th century. 5. Soldiers--Massachusetts--Northborough--History--19th century. 6. Soldiers' monuments--Massachusetts--Northborough--History--19th century. 7. Northborough (Mass.)--Biography. 8. Massachusetts--History--Civil War, 1861-1865--Personal narratives. 9. United States--History--Civil War, 1861-1865--Personal narratives. I. Title.
    F74.N9E44 2007
    974.4'303--dc22
                        2007010099

TO CHRISTINE AND MATTHEW

FOR THEIR ENCOURAGEMENT

AND PATIENCE

Contents

Acknowledgements

I have the benefit of sources unavailable to Kent or Mulligan, some of them only coming to light in 2006. In the future, more information will surface and make possible a longer and more thorough history of Northborough's part in the Civil War. In the meantime, I hope that this book is a stepping stone for any reader who would like to learn how a New England village involved itself in one of the great crises of our nation.

Several people have assisted me in this endeavor. Thomas Knoles, Marcus A. McCorison Librarian of the American Antiquarian Society, has granted permission to quote from manuscripts in the Society's collection, and staff members of that institution have been very helpful. I thank Ellen Racine, the curator of the Northborough Historical Society, where the bulk of my research has been done. She has been particularly helpful in organizing the photographs of Northborough Civil War veterans. My son, Anthony Ellis, has helped me overcome some baffling mysteries of documentation, computers and software. Christine Ellis has spent many hours reading my manuscript and suggesting improvements. Several individuals at The History Press deserve my thanks for their patient assistance, particularly Shawna Mullen and editors Greg Chalson, Saunders Robinson and Christine Langill. These people have done their part; any deficiencies that remain are mine alone.

Introduction

This history concerns the role the people of Northborough, Massachusetts, played in the American Civil War. It is well understood that the war began as a response to armed internal rebellion, but behind that rebellion lay two opposed social systems, at the heart of which was a dispute over slavery. In the North—especially in New England, and even more in Massachusetts—this dispute had been steadily and intensively scrutinized for thirty years. A case could be made that nowhere was it scrutinized more intensively than in Worcester County, Massachusetts, where the presidential candidate of the Free-Soil Party opposing the spread of slavery to the new western territories prevailed in the presidential election of 1848 and remained powerful in 1852, when nationwide support for this party dwindled. In Northborough, advocacy for this movement was even stronger. It is hardly surprising that many Southerners feared the Free-Soilers and, a few years later, the Republicans—whom they often called "black Republicans"—as relentless foes waging campaigns that they often suspected of being mere preliminaries to more profound attacks on an institution sanctioned by the federal Constitution.

I have included a discussion of the parade of abolitionists through Northborough before the war. They did not convert many citizens into abolitionists, but they fostered vigorous disapproval of the extension of slavery beyond the places where it was already established. In addition to the words of the abolitionists, a number of letters and other documents from the pre-war period reflect anti-slavery activity in town. None of these documents displays any awareness of the North's economic complicity with slavery. Like most Northern opponents of slavery, the citizens judged it a moral evil extrinsic to their own way of life but unfortunately protected by the federal Constitution. When war broke out, the soldiers of Northborough understood that they were patriots responding to the threat of disunion. The opponents were rebels; their own duty was to protect the nation. Only later did the defenders of the Union see the struggle metamorphosing into a war against slavery.

Northborough is one of many communities whose men enlisted, whose neighbors pledged support to them and their families and whose officials advanced the cause as they could. No enlistees from Northborough became famous, but many displayed bravery. Twice as many Northborough soldiers died in those four years as perished in all subsequent wars. Villagers who worked on farms and in small shops were suddenly playing their parts in a stark drama whose denouement no author had written and no participant could foresee.

The Civil War is a complex and much-studied event. Even Northborough's participation is a large subject, much of it publicly untold, some of it now untellable, but interesting diaries, letters, and other documents have come to light. Of particular importance are members of a well-educated Northborough family, the Allens, and their friends and relatives, who wrote copiously and benefited from descendents who collected and maintained their writings. I have been able to draw upon two substantial collections of this material. Much of it was not available to prior Northborough historians, and most of it has never seen print before. Wherever possible, I have drawn on the words of contemporaries—whether participants, observers or historians of military units populated by Northborough men.

Most of the details pertain to Northborough's infantry volunteers who served chiefly in the eastern region of the war: Virginia, Maryland and briefly in Pennsylvania. Artillery and cavalry volunteers have left less of a record. Previous historians have ignored the fact that a few Northborough men served in the navy; the sailors are listed in my appendix, but unfortunately, details are lacking. I recently spoke with a descendent of one of them, but she was primarily interested in and knowledgeable about his peacetime pursuits.

Two twentieth-century historians of Northborough have dealt briefly with the Civil War. In 1921, Josiah Coleman Kent published his valuable *Northborough History*, and although he diligently researched the names and records of Northborough combatants, he wrote only fourteen pages on the war. William H. Mulligan Jr.'s *Northborough: A Town and Its People, 1638–1975*, published in 1983, has a mere four pages on the war. Amazingly, there seems to be no record of any papers on the war in the century-long history of Northborough Historical Society meetings.

Northborough in 1860

Northborough stands at the eastern edge of Worcester County, Massachusetts. A stone along East Main Street, once part of the Boston Post Road, informs travelers that it is thirty-three miles from Boston. Worcester is about ten miles to the west. In 1860 there are 1,527 people in Northborough, of whom 741 are male and 786 female.[1] The most common occupation for a male is farming. The census lists no occupation at all for the great majority of females; this omission in effect signifies that many of them have the rigorous occupations of housewife and mother.

With two exceptions—a sixty-two-year-old woman named Angelina Pishaai (no occupation specified) and a fifty-two-year-old laborer, Warren Hemenway, who are listed as "mulattos"—the people are all white. Townspeople have not seen very many blacks, but a considerable number of them, in years past, have met escaped slaves.

The majority of Northborough dwellers bear what might be called Anglo-Saxon names. Two hundred nineteen of them answer to the surnames Rice, Bartlett, Brigham, Maynard, Stone, Fay, Barnes or Johnson. The only other common ethnicities are French-Canadian and Irish; nineteen Boullies and seventeen Kellys live here. The Anglo-Saxon group belongs overwhelmingly to one of the three Protestant churches in town; the Irish Americans and French-Canadian Americans are predominantly Roman Catholics.

Through the center of the village passes the Agricultural Branch Railroad, stretching a few miles north to Fitchburg and south to Framingham, a town from which you can travel just about anywhere. To go immediately east or west on the Post Road you can journey via stagecoach or by your own horse or wagon. For decades, visitors have stopped at the midtown Munroe

Tavern or a mile westward at Ball's Tavern. Recently the Northborough Inn has been erected just a stone's throw west of the Munroe Tavern, and the latter is reputed to be up for sale. There is talk that a new town hall may occupy its site. Northborough has one of the few banks in the area, a corporation consisting of three of the town's most prominent men, Cyrus Gale, George C. Davis and Wilder Bush, having founded it in 1853.[2]

Farming is the most common occupation. Some sons help on their fathers' farms and expect to inherit the farms one day or be hired by farmers; others are obliged to work in one of the town's small shoemaking establishments or one of several ornamental comb factories, which employ more workers than does a small textile mill that is making a transition from cotton to re-processed wool. Another small textile factory has burned down this year. The people who have come down from Canada—both men and women—tend to work in the textile mill; the male Irish immigrants are more often laborers or farmhands, while the women, thanks to the advantage of speaking English, often find work as domestics.

Northborough believes in education and developed a system of public elementary schools even before Massachusetts established the requirement. So far there have been three attempts at establishing a high school; the last, begun just last year, does not seem to satisfy the townspeople, and it will cease this year. A permanent high school is still a few years away. There have been several private schools in Northborough; one of them, operated by Elmer Valentine and two of his daughters, persists. There is also an establishment of adult education called the Northborough Lyceum, featuring guest speakers and debates by townsmen.

Churches are important, of course. The First Church dates from 1746. It was the major factor in the existence of Northborough as a town, for its erection established a portion of the earlier town of Westborough as a separate precinct that later became a separate town. Its pastor for the past forty-four years has been Dr. Joseph Allen, whose name and family are prominent. He is now seventy years old and has a young assistant, Trowbridge B. Forbush. Within the years of Allen's pastorate, two new congregations have formed. Just this year the Baptists have constructed a new church on Main Street. Silas Ripley is the pastor of that church, and another man whose role in this narrative will be significant, Samuel Stanford Ashley, leads the Evangelical Congregational, or, as it is usually called, the Orthodox Church. The Catholics are, as of now, without a church, so mass is celebrated in the homes of the communicants.

Some Northborough men have joined a military unit from the nearby town of Clinton. The highest-ranking Northborough man is Lieutenant

Horace Peverley was a member of the Clinton Light Guard before the war. He became a husband and father in 1860 and joined the 15th Massachusetts Infantry Regiment in 1861.

James N. Johnson; one sergeant is his younger brother, Joseph. Both are comb makers. Walter Gale, another sergeant, is a son of the richest man in town, "Captain" Cyrus Gale. He is listed as a farmer but is actually studying law. Of the two corporals from Northborough, one, Horace Peverley, married Lizzie Potter this year, and a son has already been born. Like the majority of Northborough lads, he has chosen a townsperson.[3]

The election of 1860 is a major event, with no fewer than four presidential candidates. The Democratic Party has split, with the Southern wing choosing John C. Breckinridge, the Northern choosing Stephen A. Douglas, while the Constitutional Union Party has put forward John Bell. The Republicans, offering a candidate for only the second time, have chosen an old antagonist of Douglas's, Abraham Lincoln of Illinois. The townspeople strongly support the new party, although they have heard that the Union may break apart if Lincoln is elected. In the election, however, 77 percent vote for Lincoln; the two Democrats between them attract only 9 percent of the votes.[4]

Collectively, these features do not make Northborough unique. In 1860 many towns share features like those described above, including an awareness of the issues dominating the coming election. Except for a fiercely determined but small group of people called abolitionists, people are mainly troubled by the threat of disunion. The Constitution of the United States, they understand, was written, "to form a more perfect Union." The bonds of Union joined states that argued about which powers belong to the nation and which to the states that comprise it. But an even more basic question is whether the states have the power to dissolve completely the bond of union. New Englanders' favorite candidate, Lincoln, does not think so, but several states are disagreeing with him publicly.

Behind this issue lurks one about ways of life. Americans generally—and certainly New Englanders—have for about thirty years been troubled by the variances of two modes of social organization that are characterized as Northern and Southern—and lodged at the heart of these variances is the institution of slavery. Much of what Northborough has learned about slavery has come from newspapers, some from books like Harriet Beecher Stowe's *Uncle Tom's Cabin,* and even more from a train of speakers, many of them abolitionists, at the town's lyceum. The local abolitionists, like Jairus Lincoln and Joshua Johnson, both of whom are related to the Allen family, have by their supposed excesses tended to embarrass friends and relatives.

An incident from the closing years of 1860 casts some light on this question. The youngest son of Reverend Allen, William, at this point thirty years old, is currently living in West Newton, Massachusetts. With some friends he has gone to Boston on December 15 to hear one of the great abolitionists, Wendell Phillips. He describes the experience in a letter to his sister Mary thus: "There was an evident intention to prevent him from speaking, but they found they were not strong enough, and let him go on with an occasional interruption. The Chief of Police, Coburn, sat directly behind him, policemen were concealed in all parts of the building, and the troops were under arm all the morning."[5] Allen does not describe the speech itself but tells of the aftermath when Phillips began to walk home. A dense crowd surrounded him, and the police recognized that their duty was not over. Allen and his friends, almost like children, followed the trail.

> *The policemen formed two lines through which he passed into his house, his friends gave three cheers, and the Deputy Chief briefly exhorted them to go home, adding that if the streets were not soon cleared he would clear them. This was the most exciting scene I ever witnessed, and the only time in my life I ever felt myself purposely in a position to fight, but much as I disagree with a good deal Phillips says, there is nothing we need so much to vindicate as the right of Free Speech, and the temper of the so-called Conservatives in Boston is now so fiendish that we in the country must show ourselves ready.*[6]

William Allen's behavior is ambiguous. Here is a man on his way to life as a sedentary scholar, a man for whom free speech is immensely more vital than mere emotionally violent reaction to a troublesome opponent, yet now he feels himself "in a position to fight." Is America itself now ready to fight, not *over* slavery but *because* slavery as an institution and way of life has turned a nation against itself? The decade just ended—with its stupendously ambitious but inevitably unsatisfactory Compromise of 1850, its fugitive slave legislation, its Kansas-Nebraska Act with its sectional turmoil, as well as the vigilante violence of John Brown and his men both in Kansas and at a federal arsenal in the town between the Shenandoah and the Potomac, Harper's Ferry, Virginia—this decade is a decade of strife. It is like an onion whose layers continually dilate from slavery.

How has one New England town—one of many such towns—been drawn into the struggle over slavery? Does this process—which has extended over the lifetime of a man like William Allen, born in the same year that William Lloyd Garrison's *The Liberator* was conceived, 1830—explain his conflicting feelings in the closing days of 1860? One of the attractions of these refractory abolitionists, of course, is that they put on a good show. They bring excitement and action into ordinary, often drab lives. They provoke strong negative reactions, but they are incredibly brave. It is easy to admire them even when you cannot agree with them. A man like Phillips must force observers at times to suspect their own motives. Is it perhaps only cowardice or emptiness of resolve, not prudent regard for Constitutional mandates, that holds them back? William Allen is on his way to becoming a historical scholar. Yes, free speech is more vital than fisticuffs.

On December 28 his eldest sister, Mary Allen Johnson, writes to her parents: "The times are stirring. Boston seems to be cringing. We can't tell what will come next."[7]

Chapter 1

The 1830s: Anti-Slavery Discussion Begins

W hen Joseph Allen became minister of the town's sole church in 1816, he understood that he bore a responsibility beyond what we today would think of as "religious duties." He was soon heading the school board, but public education did not necessarily lead people to a mature understanding of what life was about. So, beginning in the 1820s, he offered evening lectures in the town hall, conveniently located on the church green. The Harvard-educated minister spoke first on astronomy, a subject that townspeople probably already understood better than most of us do today. What was better to observe at night than the sky?

By 1828, Allen had extended his program considerably, as a letter from his wife Lucy to a friend makes clear:

> *Mr. Allen has delivered a course of lectures on Nat*[ural] *Theol*[ogy] *and Nat*[ural] *Hist*[ory]—*12 lectures, which have been very well attended, both by old and young, and appeared to afford great gratification, and I hope some improvement. It cost a good deal of time and labor, but Mr. Allen is amply repaid for any thing he does if he thinks it is contributing to the welfare and happiness of his family.*[8]

Natural theology and natural history pertained to observable reality—much of what we would classify as geology and biology—which Allen would have related to the unobservable. It was not Christian doctrine, but it reflected the world as a New England Christian would view it before Charles Darwin. "Family," as Mrs. Allen uses the term, surely refers not to his own household but to the townspeople he served.

Lucy Clark Ware married Reverend Joseph Allen in 1818. Mrs. Allen supervised her seven children and many students in the couple's boarding school. She listened, somewhat skeptically, to many abolitionist speakers.

Soon his lectures had blossomed into a lyceum, an institution of adult education recently developed by a Connecticut man named Jonas Holbrook in what he took to be a suitable pilot area, Worcester County, Massachusetts.[9] In December of 1828, three hundred people crammed their way into the small Northborough town hall to attend the latest lecture and debate. Originally the lyceum was the place in which Aristotle taught Greeks in the fourth century BC. Whoever designed the Northborough town hall, also attracted by classical antiquity, had fashioned it in the likeness of a Greek temple, most likely a wooden temple.[10] One of Allen's favorite topics was temperance, but speakers came and told townspeople about geology, the human voice, legerdemain, capital punishment—all sorts of subjects.

The debates which closed the meetings were usually on different subjects. Townspeople argued whether an organized militia was necessary for the safety of the country, whether interest on money should be regulated by law, whether forceful resistance to government is justifiable, whether a retired or social life is more favorable and whether men or women have greater influence in forming the character of society. Such topics elicited enthusiastic and often jocular responses. On the influence of women, a local newspaper ruled that the women seemed to come out ahead, although the reporter suggested that "gallantry" rather than conviction motivated the males.[11]

On the first day of 1831 the first issue of *The Liberator* appeared in Boston. Its originator, a twenty-five-year-old printer from Newburyport, Massachusetts, William Lloyd Garrison, was also a writer—a writer who asserted a "need to be all on fire, for I have mountains of ice about me to melt."[12] This ice was the indifference to slavery in the United States. Up to this time the most relentless opponents of slavery had been the Quakers, their most eloquent spokesman John Greenleaf Whittier of Haverhill, Massachusetts, who at the age of twenty-three edited the *New England Weekly Review* in Hartford, Connecticut. The fiery Garrison blossomed as the greatest early speaker against slavery, Whittier the greatest abolitionist writer in the 1830s.

These men were not, like so many of those "icy" individuals whom Garrison had resolved to melt, simply voices against the expansion of slavery; they wanted to end it. Resolutes like Garrison and Whittier inspired other young men—and eventually young women—to speak publicly on the subject of slavery. Many views on the subject were heard, but abolitionists turned on their heat in the meeting halls in New England, making some converts, but, more importantly, making slavery a great public issue. It is unclear whether Garrison visited Northborough or not, but many of his followers did. By the mid-1830s slavery was by far the favorite lyceum topic.

Early in 1835, fifteen-year-old Mary Allen, the oldest of the Allen children, who had already been keeping a journal for years, attended the lyceum. On January 14, she heard a lecture against slavery, "altho' it was rainy and very bad walking." One week later another speaker appeared. The process of her mind on these occasions is worth perusing.

> *Mr. Russell of West Boylston gave another lecture on slavery. It was very good, but he said too much against the colonization society. It is painful to think how many of our fellow-beings are despised merely on account of their complexion. I do not see why one who has a black skin should*

not be treated civilly at least, and it seems from Mr. Russell's account that they are not. They have a soul, and they have tender feelings, as their white bretheren [sic]. I do not think they are equal to whites <u>now</u>, but it is because they have been degraded, and their energies have been cramped by the cruel chain of slavery. They have no advantages, they can receive no education, for they have a black skin! There surely can be no intelligence, no mind beneath that skin! No! all is dark without, and all must be dark within. I never used to care for the blacks. I used to say "I am <u>sick</u> of <u>slavery</u>, or of the sound of it," but now I begin to feel more interested in them. The Town House was crowded this evening, it has not been so full for a long time. There were some from out of town, I wish there had been some from the South.[13]

Lyceum evenings often linked a lecture on one topic with a debate on another matter. On February 15, 1837, the lecturer attacked the "loathsome weed, tobacco." Participants then debated the question "Is it expedient to memorialize Congress on the subject of slavery in the District of Columbia?" The young reporter did not summarize the argument, concluding that he could not "decide which has the greater weight." At the following meeting the scheduled question was shelved in favor of a continuation of the debate on slavery in the District of Columbia.[14]

Slavery became an even more pointed topic later that year. On November 2, 1837, a local carpenter, Samuel Fisher, heard a woman named Mary White from the adjoining town of Boylston lecture on slavery at a meeting not in the lyceum but under Baptist auspices.[15] But only ten days after Mrs. White spoke, the town approved an article "to have the use of the Town Hall to hold lectures on 'Slavery.'" This seems to have been the inevitable location of such events thereafter. What Mrs. White said is not reported, but her diary from 1836 and 1837, now in the possession of the Sturbridge Village library, is peppered with notes of her attendance at anti-slavery meetings.[16] Soon Fisher was doing the same.

A few days later a shocking event spurred the anti-slavery movement. A St. Louis printer named Elijah Lovejoy, though recommending no more than a *gradual emancipation* from slavery, had been forced to flee across the Mississippi to Alton, Illinois. However, on November 7, a mob attacked his new printing plant and killed Lovejoy.

On December 5 we find Fisher and his wife at Worcester for a convention called by Worcester County ministers to discuss slavery. Joseph Allen, because of his wife's illness, could not attend the convention, but Daniel Emerson, the pastor of the Evangelical Congregational, or "Orthodox" Church, brought Allen's letter of support with him.[17] Two weeks later, son of Providence Colledge preached

18 in Shop turning bobbins &c 1/2 day

19 in do do do 1/2 day
went and herd a Lecture on
Slavery in the Town hall by
Rev Mr Phelps of Boston after
which there was an Anti
Slavery Society formed
Nahum Fisher here to day

20 in Shop made a box for A. Ball

21 in Shop work on Loom &c for self

22 in Shop work on Looms &c

23 in Shop work on do &c

24 Sunday at meeting Mr Jameson the

25 1st day Christmas verry pleasant
" and moderate
" in Shop work on Looms 1/2
" went with my wife to Nahum
" Fishers this evening

26 in Shop work on looms 3/4 day
" went to an Anti Slavery meeting in
" evening for the chose of officers
Turn over 23

A wheelwright and cabinet builder, Samuel Fisher helped establish the Northborough Anti-Slavery Society in 1837, as this diary page indicates.

after hearing Reverend Amos A. Phelps lecture at the Northborough town hall, Fisher and a number of prominent townsmen formed an anti-slavery society.[18] Northborough was doing nothing unusual; some other New England communities had already done so. Emerson was elected president; Fisher became what he called a "manager."

A parade of speakers followed. Phelps came back in January. In February of 1838 Adin Ballou, who two years later would found the utopian Hopedale Community, lectured for over two hours to a full house at the town hall.[19] Phelps was what John Milton called a warfaring Christian, Ballou a pacifist; both hated slavery. The messages heard in Northborough and in other New England towns differed stylistically and even thematically. Abolitionists could be holy or unholy in their appeals. Many people found the ministerial Phelps among the more unholy.

Northborough's Baptist minister, William H. Dalrymple, also swung into action. In January of 1838 he joined an area anti-slavery convention in Worcester. On one day the following year he preached on war in the morning, slavery in the afternoon, and temperance in the evening, with the resolute Fisher apparently present each time.[20]

Chapter 2

Anti-Slavery Efforts Widen and Deepen

In the 1830s, the speakers in the Northborough Lyceum were predominantly local figures, seldom from farther away than Boston. In the following decade, the town saw and heard more far-ranging speakers, including some remarkable slaves who had escaped their masters. Listening to these speakers assisted them in hating slavery—but with few exceptions it did not make them into abolitionists. As we shall see, townspeople also began to pay attention to political events that would greatly complicate the way of life in an expanding and discordant nation.

On June 4, 1842, the Northborough Baptists issued a resolution banning three categories of persons from their communion table. The first two—a slave-holding minister or slave-holding member—were highly unlikely possibilities, but the third—an advocate of slavery—was certainly possible. Another resolution grieved that ministers as well as members of Evangelical churches were strengthening oppressors by failing to rebuke them.[21] On April 5 of that year, the most famous of escaped slaves came to Northborough. We do not know his exact subject, but we know that in January in Boston Frederick Douglass had talked on "Absolutists and Third Parties" and on "The Southern Style of Preaching to Slaves." In May, one of his topics was "The Church Is the Bulwark of Slavery."[22] At this point he was making a tour of Massachusetts villages. If he raised the latter subject in Northborough, it would not be the only anti-clerical speech that his Northborough audience heard. One thing he was not inclined to discuss was the method of his escape. As he remarked in the *Narrative of the Life of Frederick Douglass, An American Slave*, which he would publish three years after his appearance in Northborough, "I would keep the merciless slaveholder profoundly ignorant of the means of flight adopted by the slave." He was determined to lay no obstacles in the paths of those who sought to follow him to freedom.[23]

Douglass spoke in Northborough on a Friday, and the *Frederick Douglass Papers* indicate that he was due at adjacent Westborough on Saturday, at nearby Upton on Sunday, and so on, day after day, but he was invited to speak a second time in Northborough. It would, of course, have been possible for him to address both Northborough and Westborough audiences on the same day, so it seems likely that he did.

A year later Joseph Henry Allen, the minister's twenty-two-year-old son, about to begin his own ministerial career in Roxbury, received a communication from the Board of Managers of the Massachusetts Anti-Slavery Society, signed by Francis Jackson, William Lloyd Garrison, Wendell Phillips, Maria Weston Chapman, Ellis Gray Loring, Edmund Quincy, and F.I. Bowditch. The letter urged the establishment of large anti-slavery (and of course fund-raising) meetings. The group had secured Douglass, "whose personal experiences of slavery, sound judgment and eloquence, and readiness in debate fit him to be the advocate of Freedom." The letter urged the immediate collection of funds, one dollar at least from each "earnest Abolitionist."[24]

Fired by the idealism of youth, Joseph Henry sent the letter to his father:

> *I thought it might be worth while to send you this communication, to see if anything can be done. Several have been sent here. Would not it be a good plan for me to preach for it next Sunday, as that is an extra day? I mean not in doctrine but in cash. Don't you think that some dedication of the first fruit would bring a bounty upon my future labor?*[25]

Joseph Allen had attended a number of anti-slavery conferences and had even taken his wife Lucy to one not long before. But the tone of his son's letter reflects his recognition that his father was preeminently a man of peace. Probably suspecting that he had reproving thoughts about money-changers in the temple, the son did not actually suggest that his father involve his church in the fund-raising crusade. And he knew that his father, proud that his eldest son was entering the ministry, would have to admire his desire for "first fruit" in his vocation. This letter is an important meeting of generations.

Reverend Allen's response to his son, if he made one, is not on record. His own sermons were conventional. He knew that he was no longer the "town minister," and that his messages must be aimed primarily at his congregation of Unitarian Christians. What he had already done, only a few weeks after listening to Frederick Douglass that April, was take a trip South. He had returned not long before receiving John Henry's letter, for the anti-slavery appeal was dated June 13, and John Henry's undated note probably would have come to him soon afterwards. On June 12, Reverend Allen wrote "A Prosperous Journey by the Will of God," reflecting some of the ambiguous, if not contradictory, racial attitudes often found in well-intentioned Northerners.

> *I saw slavery under its most favorable copies. There is exhibited none of its deformity, and there indeed it was invested with much that was beautiful and attractive. I saw it in the bosom of a family, and there was nothing in what met the eye to distinguish it from the service to which thousands of children are subjected in our own commonwealth. The children were well-clad, well-fed, and treated with the utmost kindness and withal trained up in orderly and virtuous habits. Nor was their education neglected. They were carefully instructed and so respectful and affectionate was their behavior that I thought it might be advantageous compared with almost any children of the same age that I had ever seen.*[26]

None of this would have attracted the Anti-Slavery Society, nor for that matter his son, although the latter, if a biographical account by his grandniece many years later is accurate, remained at this point restrained in his anti-slavery activities. The minister continues in a more critical fashion:

> *But the bad influences of the institution were but too visible all around me. It was seen in those who had obtained their freedom as well as in those who were still in bondage. The former as well as the latter seemed a degraded abject race—without energy, without enterprise, many of them hanging about public houses seeking a precarious subsistence without any regular employment.*

After more observations about the "mean appearance" of slave districts, he judges that the atmosphere stifles the South:

> *The children are brought up in ignorance and with scant means of moral and religious culture. Such are the influences of slavery so far as it came under my observation. It brings with it a blight and a curse. It represses ambition. It degrades honorable labor. It strips man of more than half its worth.*

"The slave holder," he writes, "is an object of compassion." The institution "hangs about his neck like a millstone which he deems it impossible to thrust off." Such comments reflect a Northern vision. Most Southerners did not compare slavery to millstones and had no intention of thrusting it off. But most Americans of both regions would have agreed with him that slavery "is rooted in the soil…and cannot now be easily eradicated."

If Reverend Allen was more anti-slavery than abolitionist, the marriages of his sister-in-law Mary Ware and his own eldest daughter, also named Mary, brought abolitionist vigor closer perhaps than he would have preferred. His wife's sister married a man from Hingham, Massachusetts, named Jairus Lincoln, who enjoyed combining his passions for education, music and abolition. At this time, the early 1840s, he was compiling songbooks such as *Anti-Slavery Melodies for the Friends of Freedom* for the Hingham Anti-Slavery Society. At least one of the songs, a setting of Longfellow's hymn "The Slave at Midnight," he composed himself.[27] In March of 1845, by which time he had become his brother-in-law's Northborough neighbor, he had joined a committee to criticize the recent annexation of Texas, which abolitionists viewed as a handy avenue for the expansion of slavery. He would do much more along these lines.

The Texas problem was increasing the wrath of Northern Republicans, mainly cautious in their opposition to slavery in existing states but strongly against its spread into the western territories. The Compromise of 1820 had made Missouri a slave state and the land north and west of Missouri free. In 1836, a sizable chunk of Mexico had become Texas, an independent state populated by a substantial number of American citizens, but in 1844, a dark-horse Democratic candidate for the presidency made one of his campaign promises the annexation of Texas. He also had his eye on a land yet farther west: California. And James Knox Polk won the presidency.

After periods of negotiation and border skirmishes with Mexican troops along the Rio Grande, Polk asked for a declaration of war from Congress. Despite some legislative opposition, the Northborough-born Senator John Davis among the opponents, the declaration passed. It was obvious to onlookers that Texas would become a slave state. The result was a war unpopular with a large contingent of Americans. The United States prevailed—and not only Texas, but a huge new Southwest, including not just California but the territories between Texas and California that would eventually become all or most of the future states of Arizona, New Mexico, Nevada, Colorado and Utah could become American slave territory.

At the same time a new cadre of abolitionists was emerging. A young black man named William Wells Brown had escaped from slavery back in 1834, then worked as a steamboat man on Lake Erie and as an Underground Railroad agent in the area of Buffalo, New York, for the next nine years. After serving as an anti-slavery lecturer in western New York, he shifted his attention to Boston, publishing his autobiography in 1847.

William Wells Brown escaped from slavery in Kentucky in 1834, and worked as a steamboat man, conductor for the Underground Railroad, speaker and writer. A granddaughter of Reverend Allen became his friend at the age of six.

On Washington's birthday, February 22, 1848, Brown spoke in Northborough. Although we have no text of the speech, it seems likely that his talk paralleled one he had given in Salem, Massachusetts, three months earlier. This speech had been recorded by a system of phonetic shorthand. "My subject," he said, "is slavery as it is, and its influence upon the morals and character of the American people." A slave, Brown pointed out, was merely "a thing, a piece of property." He went on to anticipate a point made famous by the English aristocrat, Lord Acton, nearly forty years later: "Power tends to corrupt, and absolute power corrupts absolutely." As Brown expressed it, "Give one man power over another, and he will abuse that power; no matter if there be law; no matter if there be public sentiment in favor of the oppressed."[28] Like Reverend Allen, he judged that slavery corrupted the South, but he cited also its ruinous influence on the North. He was particularly exasperated with churches and religious organizations. When the American Anti-Slavery Society offered to underwrite the cost of sending Bibles to slaves, the American Bible Society refused to cooperate. "Has the American Tract Society ever published a single line against the sin of slaveholding?" he asked.[29]

As to the influence of slavery upon government, he noted that on the Fourth of July "orators talk of Liberty, Democracy, and Republicanism… while three millions of their own countrymen are groaning under abject slavery." Americans think that they live in the cradle of liberty, but "they have rocked the child to death." Government was working to spread slavery to the new territories. Fugitives like him lived in fear. "If I wish to stand up and say, 'I am a man,' I must leave the land that gave me birth."[30] In the conclusion of his Salem speech, he returned to his earlier characterization of the slave and summed up the charges against the nation:

> *Recollect that you have come here tonight to hear a slave, and not a man, according to the laws of the land; and if that slave has failed to interest you, charge it not to the race, charge it not to the colored people, but charge it to the blighting influences of slavery—that institution that has made me property, and that is making property of three millions of my countrymen at the present day. Charge it upon that institution that is annihilating the minds of three millions of my countrymen. Charge it upon that institution, whether found in the political arena or in the American churches. Charge it upon that institution, cherished by the American people, and looked upon as the essence of Democracy—upon American Slavery.*[31]

It was to remarks of this type that the people of Northborough also were attending.

In Northborough, Brown stayed with the family of Dr. Joshua Johnson and his wife, the former Mary Allen. Like most of the Allens, Mary had been recording her life since childhood, and one of her present activities was maintaining a journal for her children. At this time her daughter Harriet was six, Richard, her son, was only a few months old. The following is Mary's journal entry for February 27:

> *We have had in our family for two days this last week a fugitive slave who is lecturing here and in the vicinity. Before he came, Harriet seemed for some reason or other to have a 'prejudice against color.' The first night he was here she refused to shake hands with him, and would not bid him good night. I asked her why she did not shake hands with Mr. Brown. She said, 'Why mother, do I shake hands with you, when I go to bed?' 'No.' 'Then why should I shake hands with him, I'm not used to it.' They became great friends before he went away, and she was evidently very much surprised to see so light complexioned a man, for she had only seen a very few black Negroes in the street and seemed to think the color would come off, like crock. She said to me, 'Why mother, I don't think Mr. Brown is very black'—and then she called me to her & whispered, 'but his hair!'*[32]

Harriet would have another chance to meet her friend Mr. Brown, but before that happened, Northborough, like other American towns, was responding to the political situation of 1848. President Polk had endured but had little enjoyed the rigors of his term, and he made clear that he would retire thereafter. His would-be Democratic successor, Lewis Cass, believed that Westerners should choose slavery or freedom for themselves, while the Whigs lined up behind General Zachary Taylor, a slave-owning Southern Whig.

To men like Jairus Lincoln, the apolitical Taylor—who seemed willing to accept Northern Whigs' opposition to extending slavery into the West—was not a safe bet. One hundred and seventy-two men of the town, "disgusted with the nominations for President and Vice-president," wrote a petition demanding "the nomination of independent candidates…who are KNOWN to be opposed to the further extension of Slavery, and in favor of its immediate abolition in any District or Territory belonging to the United States." The signers included Lincoln and Dr. Johnson, of course, but also many other prominent men of the town, including Joseph Allen. The petition is undated, but it seems to have preceded the nomination of former president Martin Van Buren as the candidate of the new Free-Soil Party.

This group, styling themselves "The Free-Soil Crew" presented one hundred lines of doggerel verse composed and sung by Jairus Lincoln at a free-soil meeting in Northborough, immediately prior to Election Day. The tune, *Dandy Jim*, begins:

> *As Free Soil men we're gathered here;*
> *The Cass men sure we cannot fear;*
> *The Taylor men to Zach belong,*
> *We're freemen and are therefore strong.*
> *We have the numbers, have the might,*
> *We're for freedom, we are right,*
> *We to every class belong,*
> *With the people's strength we're strong.*[33]

The first few days of November were a political cauldron. On November 8, Lucy Allen wrote a long letter to her daughter Elizabeth:

> *Four nights last week our people went to meetings in the neighboring towns—Westboro, Shrewsbury, Grafton, and Worcester…Mr. Lincoln has a famous free soil song wh[ich] he has manufactured for the occasion and alters to suit the circumstances of the different places. There was a great gathering at Worcester Sat evening…The Whigs sent for Webster to put down free soil and boasted that it was almost dead. They obtained the city hall which holds 3000, and the Freesoilers were obliged to take the Depot which holds 3500.*[34]

As she saw it, "there was no enthusiasm in the Whig meetings." Town voters did not like General Taylor, despite the fact that he evinced no interest in promoting slavery (although he himself was a slave owner). The Allens generally seemed inclined to regard Taylor as the most favorable possibility, but the result in Northborough was resoundingly otherwise. The former Democrat, Martin Van Buren, the Free-Soil candidate, received 188 votes, Taylor only 64 and Democratic Louis Cass just 24. Although the vote was closer in Worcester County, it too proved a hotbed of Free-Soil voters; Van Buren received 8,634 votes, Taylor only 6,008.[35] Yet nationwide, Van Buren received less than 10 percent of the votes. Taylor won and attempted to fend off hotheads of all persuasions.

Because of the recent discovery of gold in California, he agreed that it should become a state. California prohibited slavery, however, at a time when the thirty existing states were equally divided—fifteen slave states and fifteen free states. Southerners saw the political balance of power tipping against

THE FREE SOIL CREW.

Sung at a Free Soil Meeting at Northborough, Nov. 11, 1848.

COMPOSED AND SUNG BY JAIRUS LINCOLN. Tune—Dandy Jim.

I.

As Free Soil men we're gathered here ;
The Cass men sure we cannot fear ;
The Taylor men to Zack belong,
We're freemen, and are therefore strong.
We have the numbers, have the might,
We're for freedom, we are right,
We to every class belong,
With the people's strength, we're strong.

II.

We've picked our crew, we've hoisted sail,
We chose for captain Cyrus Gale,
For he has freely signed our call
With Joseph and with Baker Ball.
We've for our pilots, Foster Shaw,
And he's enlisted for the war,
With Haynes and Coburn Henry G,
Instead of Wilder, Warren T.

III.

Our mate are Abraham, William, Sam,
They'll drink no grog, but they'll eat ham ;
Instead of Nahum or his son,
We'll have for clerk our Crawford John.
Let Barnes and Johnson surgeons be,
But they must serve without a fee,
As surgeons' mates we've Phelps and Gray,
With Lewis and with Abraham Fay.

IV.

And that we ne'er be in the dark,
We'll have for counsel, Samuel Clark,
And for our boatswain, Davis James,
He soon shall see the river Thames.
We want as mates two young men brisk,

We've no one yet to man the top,
Cries Potter, and I will not stop,
With Merrick I will take my stand
With Miles and Wood, a fearless band.

IX.

Says Maynard James, and Caleb too,
With Haven, we are of the crew,
Cries Silas Allen, " come on board,"
And on the deck a host was poured.
There's Jonathan Bailey, Fabian ?
Holloway Bailey, true man he,
Abel Warren, never wrong,
Martin Rice, both sound and strong.

X.

Are Hunt and Stacy, Lincoln here,
Or Holman from the red house near ?
Let's call the list before we part ;
Where's Whittemore and Dr. Hart ?
Now if we're ever in a pinch,
There's younger Gale, or Stone, or Winch,
But Stephen Jerauld is the one
That's missing with his noble son.

XI.

Cries Stephen Jerauld,—I'm not last ;
See Ball and Bruce, they're coming fast ;
There's Jonas Babcock, Parker John,
With Johnson Charles, and Johnson Tom.
Our fathers, Eager, Stratton, bold
Like Cawthorne D, the truth have told,
And Freeman, though he's at the mill,
Like Coxon, he's a freeman still.

XII.

This "Free-Soil" song was a composition of Reverend Allen's brother-in-law, Jairus Lincoln, a fierce opponent of slavery who moved to Northborough from Hingham, Massachusetts in the early 1840s.

their region, and saw the danger of the same thing happening in New Mexico Territory. Taylor was undoubtedly relieved to see Senator Henry Clay of Kentucky organizing what became known as the Compromise of 1850, which brought on the famous debate amongst several senators: Clay, Thomas Hart Benton of Missouri, John C. Calhoun of South Carolina, and a man whom the voters of Massachusetts hoped they could trust, Daniel Webster. Calhoun, fighting for the Southern cause, but a lover of the Union, was almost exactly correct in predicting secession within ten years. In the midst of this debate, both Calhoun and Tayor died, the former in March, the latter in July. The Compromise, an attempt to appease both North and South, proved more expeditious than effectual and led to further wrangles.

Back in Northborough early in 1849, William Wells Brown returned with two recently escaped slaves, William and Ellen Craft. Harriet's grandmother, Lucy Allen, first mentions them in a letter to her daughter Elizabeth, then away from home, on January 17, 1849.

> *I heard last night of the most interesting case of escape from slavery I think that I have ever heard of—a man and his wife have just arrived in Boston from Georgia. She is almost perfectly white—and the way they effected their escape was this. They had been able to lay up a good deal of money—being capable and industrious—and she drest in men's clothes and personated the master, which as she was so white she was well able to do—and her husband was the slave. They traveled openly and put up at the most public hotels on the way—and as they could neither of them write and would be obliged to scribe their names sometimes, she kept her hand wrapped up as if it was lame, and he would not be expected to write—of course. In this way they have at last reached our free soil—which I hope they will find a free land for them. This for wretches who do not know how to take care of themselves is quite an achievement.* [36]

Lucy Allen wrote hundreds, probably thousands, of letters and they usually provide precise details. Her recollection of William and Ellen Craft's Northborough appearance accords with the Crafts' own version of their story which he related later in a book called *Running a Thousand Miles for Freedom.* In another letter to Elizabeth dated February 20, 1849, she seems to have forgotten that she has already written about the Crafts in her January 17 letter. She also has learned a good deal more about how the Crafts "take care of themselves."

> *I suppose you have seen some account in the papers of some slaves who escaped from Georgia. We had them in town last week and held a meeting to hear their story. W.W. Brown was with them, and they spent the night at Dr. Johnson's [i.e., her son-in-law's] home. They were very much interested and pleased with them. Harriet was delighted to see Mr. Brown again and paid him every attention. He made a few remarks at first and then introduced the man to tell his own story, which he did in a very simple and straight forward way and with a great deal of shrewdness and dry humor. He said nothing at all respecting slavery itself or of his situation*

in it, but merely related the story of his escape, which the more I think of, the more remarkable I think it.[37]

In sponsoring this couple Brown did not think the Crafts' account of their escape as damaging to the prospects of later escapees, for he undoubtedly judged it unique and inimitable. The letter continues:

The more wonderful I think their self-possession and fast thought and resources. He is a cabinet maker, who was valued by his master, as he said in answers to questions at $1,500. He received 34 dollars a month, out of which he paid his master 220 a year, and boarded and clothed himself and partly his wife, and laid by enough to get away. He is about 24 and had always had his eye on Freedom and soon began to provide for it, as you may suppose…She was the ladies' maid of her mistress, seamstress &c. and her mistress would not take any price for her. They thought about 3 months ago that the time had come, and for a month, he said, they scarcely slept for excitement and anxiety. He said they chose this time of year because they w[ou]ld be less likely to meet with those who know them. He said in his shrewd way that most persons when they travelled like to meet with their acquaintances, but he preferred to leave his behind. He gave an amusing account of the manner in which he provided his wife with a suit of man's apparel, including a pair of green gloves wh[ich] he said he bought for a cousin who had very sore eyes, so the man, pleased with his kindness, let him have them cheap.

Lucy Allen, as we shall see, was not the only person to recognize and exemplify William Craft's resourcefulness and shrewd wit. Many people well disposed toward blacks felt more pity than hopefulness about their future, as if one could not expect such qualities. Whatever Mrs. Allen's former thoughts about the capacities of African Americans, she obviously found both his story and manner of relating it "wonderful." The next sentence of her letter records a fact that suggests another aspect of the Crafts' planning. They apparently knew that Philadelphia had a longstanding reputation for medical excellence. Several of the following details also reflect the extent of their foresightedness:

They represented themselves as Mr. Johnson and his servant, going to Phila. to consult a physician on account of the master's health. She tied up her face to disguise her want of a beard, and her hand, lest she might be called upon to register her name at the hotels. They got away for 3 or 4 days under pretense of going to see an aunt of hers a few miles off. So that I suppose they were not suspected for some days. They lived but a short distance from the rail-road and walked there easily before anyone was stirring. From Savannah they took the steam boat to Charleston, intending there to take the Columbus for Phila., but they found, on arriving there that it was chartered for California, and they were obliged to come on 1000 miles through the midst of the slave states. At Charleston, they were obliged to undergo a pretty close questioning and scrutiny in the custom house from 3 of the officers, and when finally she excused herself from writing her name on account of her lame hand the captain of the vessel in wh[ich] they came did it for her. It was amusing to hear him tell of his running to get fresh poultries for his master as soon as they reached a hotel, or went onto a boat, and wearing flannels and rubbing his feet with opodeldoc, for it was inflammatory rheumatism which he was so troubled with. He would ask for a room where his master could lie down, and excuse him from eating much because he felt so bad—and he said it was true enough, he did feel bad. I suppose we can easily imagine that. The poor panting fugitives could not have had much appetite, tho' now they can make some things appear amusing in the recollection which were very far from it in passing. At one place near the end of his journey he was so beat out for want of sleep that he had got to sleep in the cars (he was in the Jim Crow car, and his master in the 1st class) when they came to a stop his master was in great consternation at his not appearing to help him out, for he was almost helpless you know. He made many inquiries and at last he appeared. His fellow travellers asked why his master was so anxious. They said they supposed he suspected him of intending to run away. Then they asked him if he intended to go back with his master. He said certainly—he loved his master too well to leave him, and he sh[ou]ld certainly go back when he did, said he, and told a good many lies to get away, but I believe that was pretty near he truth.

The following passage reflects the time, December of 1848, before the passage of the notorious Fugitive Slave Act put escaped slaves in additional peril.

They asked him if he did not know he was free as soon as he got to Phil. Yes, he said, but he could not leave his master. He heard one of them say afterward, "That nigger will never go back with his master—I see freedom in his eye," and said he, "I don't know but he [sic] did. For I began to feel it about that time." At Baltimore they had rather a searching time. They refused to let them pass without bonds signed by some person at Baltimore. As they knew no one, they had to get out of the cars and went into the ticket office (I believe). There they were subjected to a severe questioning, and on account of the state of health of Mr. Johnson and as they found they had tickets through to P. from Charleston, they finally let them pass. It was in the night. Some one in the car directed them to a colored boarding house in Phila[delphia] *so there they had no trouble. And there they met W.W. Brown, who persuaded them to come here instead of going to Canada as they intended. And now I hope their troubles are over, and they will reap the reward of their enterprise. They are going to settle down in Worcester. I think this cold season must be very trying to them. Such a contrast to Georgia.*

Before concluding Lucy Allen's letter, it might be appropriate to summarize the Crafts' future life, which has been ably told by R.J.M. Blackett in his edition of *Running a Thousand Miles to Freedom*. They settled in Boston, rather than Worcester, and worked in their vocations as cabinetmaker and seamstress. Although nominally safe, they feared that because of the publicity they had attracted, some attempt might be made to capture them and return them to their Georgia master. The Massachusetts Anti-Slavery Society vowed to protect them, but the passage of the Fugitive Slave Act in 1850 destroyed their hopes that troubles were over. They immediately fled to Canada. Soon thereafter they decided to live in England, where they and several other black Americans, including William Wells Brown, worked to gain British support for the battle against American slavery. By 1860 the now-literate William Craft published his account of their venture in London. Later he went to Dahomey (now Benin, immediately west of Nigeria) to work against the slave trade still being practiced there. In 1869, the Crafts moved back, not just to the United States, but to Georgia. At a place called Hickory Hill they purchased a plantation; Ellen and her daughter ran schools for children in the day and for adults at night. But in the fall of 1870, after their house and barn were burned by nightriders, they retreated to Savannah, where their son Charles operated a boarding house. Then they tried another plantation called Woodville, which had been destroyed during the war. Ellen continued to teach, and they persevered over the years despite many financial and social difficulties. She died in 1892. Eventually William's plantation fell into the hands of a fertilizer company, and he died at his daughter's home in Charleston, South Carolina.

Lucy Allen's long letter ends thus:

After he had told his story many asked him questions. His answers were wonderfully ready and shrewd—almost as if he had known them

The intelligence and resourcefulness of fugitive slaves William and Ellen Craft captivated Lucy Allen, as this excerpt from one of her letters reveals.

beforehand. He said he had been so long thinking of getting away that he did not want to take a common way. I don't know when I have been so excited and interested in any thing—to see them and hear their simple and thrilling story and think what must have been their feelings for these many weeks to be sure their actual sufferings were not great, but their wish was as great and perhaps greater than most. They had counted the cost and knew what they sh[ou]ld have to suffer if taken. He ended by saying he hoped we sh[ou]ld excuse the manner of getting away—he meant using so much deception. Some one said yes, if you won't do it again. He answered that he hoped he sh[ou]ld not have occasion to but if he had, he rather thought he should, and who would blame them. Does not the very fact of their being able to carry thro' as they did such a course of deception and lay their plans with much art show as plainly as anything one of the hideous faces of Slavery. But I will let you make y[ou]r own reflection.

One more recollection of the Crafts' visit to Northborough exists, written in September of 1911 by another Allen. Horatio Allen seems to have been one of several relatives of Reverend Allen who found their way from the town of Medfield, about twenty miles southeast of Northborough. He attended the Allens' boarding school for a time and worked in one of the town's comb factories. Writing from Petershaven, which must have been a retirement or nursing home in Roxbury, Connecticut, sixty-two years later, undoubtedly in response to a request by Harriet Hall Johnson—who by this time was herself a woman in her late sixties and an active member of the Northborough Historical Society. Horatio, in the trembling hand of an old man, recalled another of the questions that William Craft had fielded so neatly. "One person asked, 'Were you not treated well by your master?' 'Yes.' 'Why then did you run away?' 'My place is vacant, and you can have it if you wish.'"[38] The point, of course, is that thoughtful blacks did not want to be "treated" at all. To be treated with "kindness," to be trained in "orderly and virtuous habits" meant to be properly docile and obedient to white masters and mistresses. Of course adults took for granted that all children would be "respectful and affectionate" to their elders. But men like William Wells Brown and William Craft recognized the extra dimension in the instruction of African Americans. White children would grow up to be white adults; black children would still be slaves. Horatio Allen also recalled seeing Douglas, Brown, Stephen S. Foster, C.C. Burleigh "and other pioneers [who] advocated the cause of the slave."

Most likely as a consequence of the influence of Jairus Lincoln, the senior Allen's son-in-law, Dr. Joshua J. Johnson, was recognized as a supporter of a new batch of abolitionist speakers eager to spread the word to every possible hamlet. One of these, Stephen S. Foster, wrote to Johnson urging (and the emphasis is his) *"a genuine, thoroughgoing…Disunion Convention."*[39] This radical version of abolitionism—the casting off of slave states—frightened not only the processors of Southern cotton and other economic ties between North and South but many who despised slavery.

Foster coolly invited himself to Northborough on Friday, June 13, which he said fit in nicely with a scheduled appearance in adjoining Marlborough on the two prior evenings. He came, talked and left a record—rather a

"The anti-slavery movement overwhelmed all other topics," wrote Horatio Allen, as he recalled in old age his visits to anti-slavery lectures in Northborough.

stormy one—in Northborough. He had first appeared in town on January 12, 1848, several weeks before Brown's initial visit. Not to be confused with his younger, song-writing contemporary, Stephen Collins Foster, this man struck some of his listeners as one of the most fanatical of anti-slavery speakers. He informed his hostess that it was her "duty to give up the church." At one of his appearances Foster was "grossly insulted" by his audience, in the words of a diarist to which Harriet Johnson (but not the present writer) had access. A subsequent meeting to discuss, perhaps to prepare, an apology, met with little success because few people attended.[40] Other accounts of Foster's effect on audiences also testify to his talent for infuriation. His wife, Abigail Kelley Foster, more than once incited mob violence when she lectured on abolition, temperance and women's rights.

Both Fosters bristled with anti-clerical and anti-government sentiments trying to many of those who invited them. She also spoke in Northborough, although no anecdotes of her reception remain.

Writing again to daughter Elizabeth only three days after her long and enthusiastic account of the Crafts' impact, Lucy Allen describes her dilemma:

> *You know that I told you that some of y*[ou]*r father's sermons were rather odious in the eyes of some —and they say he is influenced by the Dr.* [Johnson] *and Mr. Lincoln, and they have both made themselves very unpopular by their peculiar manner of advocating their side of the question.* [The following sentence is Mrs. Allen's interlinear addition.] *You know they are both of them rather overbearing. They little know how many battles he fights with them and how truly he sympathizes with them in some of their strange notions. But as they are son* [in-law] *and brother-in-law he must help bear the odium of their doings. Well, it must be confessed: a minister's life is a hard one.*[41]

CR⊗SO

The 1850s produced, for Northborough and the nation, a string of unsettling events beginning with the Compromise, with its more rigorous fugitive slave law, which bred more intense opposition from the Underground Railroad. No authentic information has come to light establishing any specific Northborough stops on this network, but they must have existed because a Northborough comb maker named Calvin Cook is known to have conveyed refugees to stops in Leominster, Massachusetts, about fifteen miles northward.[42]

In 1854, townspeople heard much about an escaped black man, Anthony Burns, who was captured in Boston. The legally sound attempt to remove him and return him to his Virginia master aroused so much anger that it took eight artillery units and the full force of the Boston police to usher Burns out of the city.

The Kansas-Nebraska Act of 1854 led to violence which Jairus Lincoln projected in a drama he wrote for a performance at the Northborough Lyceum, now converted into a "Young Man's Lyceum." Called *Life in Kansas*, it was enacted in Westborough on April 12, 1855, rather than in Northborough, perhaps because of local opposition to Lincoln's ferocity. The text of this play has not survived, but a program indicates that some of its characters—Governor Reeder, Sutton (slaveholder), George (his son), LeGree, Officer, and "slave to Sutton"—suggest Lincoln's interpretation

EXHIBITION

—— OF THE ——

NORTHBORO

YOUNG MEN'S LYCEUM,

AT THE TOWN HALL, WESTBORO,

On Thursday Evening, April 12th, 1855.

PROGRAMME.

1. Prologue, - W. D. Burdett.
(Written by J. Lincoln.)

2. THE VILLAGE SQUIRE.

Uncle Tim,	C. F. Babcock	Jonathan,	J. H. Allen
Edgarston,	J. N. Johnson	Millwood,	J. M. Wood

3. THE SAILOR'S RETURN.
(Written by J. Lincoln.)

Sailor,	-	F. Leach	Parent, - M. G. Rice

4. EDITORIAL COMFORTS.

Editor, - - - -	C. B. Johnson
Printer's devils, - -	John Jones and A. Fay
Loafer, - - - -	John M. Wood
Farmer, - - - -	Charles Potter
Patron, - - - -	C. F. Babcock

5. THE BELLS, - W. D. Burdett

6. THE HATTER AND PRINTER.

Bouncer, - , Charles Potter	Felter, -	W. D. Burdett
Printer, - - -		J. P. Wheeler

7. LIFE IN KANSAS.
(Written by J. Lincoln.)

Governor Reeder, - - -	C. B. Johnson
Zeek, - - - -	Cyrus Potter
Sutton, (slaveholder,) - -	M. G. Rice
George, (his son,) - -	F. T. Leach
LeGree, - - - -	H. Glazier
Atchinson, - - -	W. D. Burdett
Chairman of Committee, - -	Charles Potter
Secretary, - - -	A. Forrester
Officer, - - -	J. N. Johnson
Slave to Sutton, - -	Anthony D. Burns

Closing Address, - - W. D. Burdett
(Written by J. Lincoln.)

In this Northborough Lyceum program of 1855 one can see the
names of several future soldiers in the anti-slavery play *Life in Kansas*.

of the real-life drama existing in that troubled territory after the Kansas-Nebraska Act of 1854. In addition to "LeGree,"—Lincoln's obvious attempt to imitate Harriet Beecher Stowe's Simon Legree—the name of one of the actors, Anthony D. Burns, sounds suspiciously like a pseudonym meant to remind the audience of the man recently carted back to Virginia under provisions of the Fugitive Slave Act of 1850.[43] The following year Massachusetts Senator Charles Sumner delivered a three-day speech called "The Crime against Kansas" in which he attacked the sponsors of the act, Stephen A. Douglas and Andrew P. Butler. Two days later Preston S. Brooks, a South Carolina congressman who was also Butler's nephew, attacked Sumner in the Senate chamber, beating him with a cane so severely that it put Sumner out of commission for three years. Among the reactions was that of Joseph Henry Allen, by this time the pastor of a church in Bangor, Maine. He now had no need to ask his father's opinion about what he should do. His sermon on June 1, based on Luke 21:26, "Men's hearts failing them for fear, and for looking after those things which are coming on the earth," is entirely about the violence of the time.

> *Two years ago, the experiment of popular sovereignty so called—that is, the right to carry slavery into territory declared by solemn compact for ever free—was set on foot in defiance of a voice of remonstrance that went up like low thunder from the whole horizon of the North. At this moment that experiment is a ghastly and bloody failure…The fair fields of the fertile West are overrun by a mob of armed and drunken plunderers, and red with the blood of murdered men.[44]*

After reviewing the assault on Sumner, whom Allen knew personally, for he had practiced his ministry for several years in Washington, he told his congregation that "now, we are told, the majority of Congress carry weapons to their seats. Representatives in a free Republic go armed against one another, in little knots and companies in the street." Slave people, he charged, "choose the open terrors of a blood fight." Of course Allen did not ask his congregation to respond in kind, but urged "freedom of thought and speech." His talk, loosely hung on a biblical text, was more anti-slavery tract than sermon.

Then came the Dred Scott decision of 1857, denying the citizenship of African Americans and, two years later, John Brown's attack on Harper's Ferry. By the end of that year Brown had been hanged, and bitterness against abolitionists had elevated even more. The last decade before the outbreak of war was a bitter one for both Northern and Southern Americans.

Chapter 3

Northborough Enters the War

A week after war erupted, Lucy Allen's eldest daughter, Mary, wrote to her from the Johnson family's present home in Keene, New Hampshire. "I feel that I could almost consent to send a dear friend to fight for our country, for the war seems a necessary one and quite as much for principle, as the revolutionary war."[45] Mary's husband was nearly fifty-two, her only two sons (both of whom would die that year) only five and eighteen months old, respectively, but she certainly did have dear friends who were eligible.

The first Northborough enlistee, and perhaps the most unusual one, was Charles B. Farwell, who enlisted in the 2nd Massachusetts Regiment in March before the attack on Fort Sumter. Discharged in September, he rejoined in August of 1862 as a resident of Boylston, Massachusetts, served nearly ten months, was again discharged, and finally, as a resident of Worcester, served again in the early months of 1865.[46] The other Northborough enlistments did not begin until July.

After Confederate troops seized Fort Sumter, the federal military fortress in the harbor near Charleston, South Carolina, on April 14, President Lincoln asked for fifty thousand militia troops to serve for three months, hoping that in that period of time the leaders of seven Southern states—South Carolina, Mississippi, Florida, Alabama, Georgia, Louisiana and Texas—who claimed to have seceded from the Union would see the error of their ways. Instead, Virginia, North Carolina, Arkansas and Tennessee took the same course. Neither then nor later did Lincoln recognize this action as true secession.

As Southerners saw it, he had challenged a fixed and stable way of life. The president had asserted that his office gave him no power to end slavery in the states where it already existed. Many Northerners, especially many citizens of Massachusetts, had opposed the spread of slavery beyond those states. By this time the Free-Soil party had failed; the new hope was the Republican Party, with Lincoln its second presidential candidate and its first successful one. But the ferocity of abolitionists, John Brown's assault on the federal arsenal at Harper's Ferry, and Southern distrust of Lincoln warned the Confederates not to submit to a Northern Republican government. An anti-slavery man today might turn into an ardent abolitionist tomorrow.

In a major battle at a small stream called Bull Run, near the town of Manassas, Virginia, in July of 1861, many men were killed, and the federal army retreated ignominiously. As a result, Congress authorized another five hundred thousand troops—not for three months this time, but for three years. By the end of July, twenty-three men between the ages of fifteen and forty had enlisted from Northborough. Seven more left home in August, sixteen in September.[47] Many a woman was hugging a son, brother, lover or husband good-bye.

In September, one of the new soldiers was Warren F. Eames. Eames was eighteen years old, the most common age of these recruits. We know little of his life before 1861, although copies of two school essays from a few years earlier exist.[48] In one of them the ten-year-old Warren recommends that all facing a difficult task should "say 'I'll try,' and the work is done." Now he would try to help subdue the recalcitrant South. His father, Christopher Columbus Eames, who in 1848 had signed the petition for a party that would ban the extension of slavery, kept a diary in which he occasionally jotted down something he wanted to remember about his farm or the carpentry that he also practiced. His entry of Tuesday, September 3, 1861, was for him a long one, but the occasion was special: "Arrived in Boston & went out to Reedville & saw Warren for the last time before he went to Washington to fight the Rebels (arrived home today)."[49]

Warren had joined the Union Army four days earlier. Meanwhile his father and younger brother John were traveling to Mount Washington and across the Maine-New Hampshire border into Newry, Maine, the family's home town before moving to Northborough when Warren was a small boy. Columbus and John then went directly to Boston and then a few miles south to Readville, where the 20th Massachusetts Infantry Regiment was being organized. After their farewells, letters passed between Warren and his family. His unit moved to Poolesville, Maryland, about twenty-five miles up the Potomac River from Washington. A couple of miles beyond a bluff across the river in Leesburg, Virginia, Rebel troops were poised under the command of Colonel Nathan G. Evans, an 1848 graduate of the United

States Military Academy, and known as a hard drinker—but also as a leader who had commanded his brigade notably at Bull Run.

Of Colonel Evans and his brigade Warren Eames probably knew little, but he expressed supreme confidence in a letter he wrote to his father on September 9. "I don't see what need there is of staying here on this side any longer…I think we could knock the whole of them into Kingdom Come, if they would only let us cross and go at them."[50] He noted that he had run into two fellow townsmen, both members of the 15th Massachusetts Regiment. Charles Warren was his own age, eighteen, and Tom Woodward Jr., a few years older, lived on Main Street, only a few hundred yards west of the Eames farm.

Soldiers were not always in the mood to "go at" them. Before continuing with Warren Eames's letter, we might note that the enemy had a lot in common with their Northern counterparts, not merely wounding, capturing, or killing them. The following undated note, possibly referring to Smart's Mill at Ball's Bluff, found its way into the Civil War collection of the Northborough Historical Society.

> *Gents of the U.S. Army*
>
> *Compliments of the Rebels. By their <u>Packet</u> they send you a few pieces of the luxuriant weed and some papers. In return we request of you some coffee, papers and a deck of cards if you have them. We will send you this morning's papers as soon as they arrive. We loaded a boat yesterday with papers and tobacco but the 'contraption' capsized. Reverse the rudder and Main sheet so that the boat may land at a point just below the mill race.*
>
> *Mississippians*[51]

There were certainly Mississippians in the Confederate contingent across the Potomac from the Massachusetts 20th Regiment.

To return to Eames's letter home, the men of his own regiment had been told, he said, to fill their canteens and be ready to march.

> *The next day, they said we were to cross the river that night with 16 other regiments; but we did not go…However, we were roused up and 4 of our companies sent to the ferry, as they expected an attack from rebel cavalry. So we went down at 10 o'clock and stood around awhile, and then went into a forsaken old store and lay down anywhere we could. I lay, a part of the time, on a counter; and a part I got on a dry goods shelf. Lucky I was, as many had to lie on the dirty floor. That was the first building I had been in since I left Washington.*[52]

After noting that he was in Company D, "the left flank company, the second post of honor," he promised to "write again soon. Respects to all."

Columbus Eames, a busy and prosperous man in Northborough, always found time to compose Sunday letters to his son. Receiving no further replies, he wrote on Tuesday, October 22, only two days after his most recent one. On that evening the first report came. After noting in his diary the record of his own eighth letter to Warren, he wrote: "He[a]rd at 7 PM of the Battle at Balls Bluff." Three anxious days later, more ominous news arrived. "Got a List of the killed wounded & missing in the Battle at Balls Bluff. Warren reported <u>missing</u>."[53]

At some later time Columbus Eames wrote, under the date of Monday, October 21, "Battle at Leesburg or Balls Bluff in which Warren was <u>Lost</u>." After receiving the list, it did not take Warren's father long to determine what to do. He borrowed $100 from the Northborough Bank and on October 26 "started for Pool[e]sville to learn what I could of Warren."

On Sunday at 5:00 a.m. the senior Eames, presumably traveling by train, arrived in New York and went to Brooklyn to hear the most famous minister of the day, and a noted abolitionist, Henry Ward Beecher. The next morning Eames left New York for Baltimore, a trip that took thirteen hours. On Tuesday he reached Washington and set forth for Poolesville, arriving at Camp Benton at 4:30 p.m.

"Make enquires all day about Warren," he wrote the next day. Two companies, one of them Warren's Company D of the 20th Massachusetts Regiment, had been the first to cross the river at 4:00 on the morning of October 21 on what was originally intended to be a reconnaissance mission but became an engagement for which the inexperienced federal troops were unprepared. By 7:30 p.m., after several blunders and missed signals, the Northern troops had been whipped and driven back like the Union men at Bull Run three months earlier.[54] The men whom Columbus Eames was questioning, of course, bore the scars of a perilous day of battle on the evening of which they had raced down the bluff to the shore and successfully swam to, or, in a few cases, found vehicles to carry them to Harrison's Island, while Mississippi riflemen fired down on them from above.

Company D, including Eames and four other Northborough men, had been heavily engaged; Thomas Burdett, John Stearns, Levi Whitcomb and Josiah Proctor had returned, but some of these men were now in a hospital in Washington. Columbus Eames's account for October 30 concludes: "Find he was badly wounded in the mouth but those best qualified to judge think it is not a fatal wound and that he is a prisoner, but I think it very likely he is dead." Eames probably judged that the soldiers were offering him the

Here is evidence of attempted comradery between Mississippi men and Northern soldiers, probably at Ball's Bluff.

boat yesterday with papers
and Tobacco but the
"Contraption" capsised
Reverse the rudder and
main sheet so that
the boat may land
at a point just below
the Mill race *

Missippians

* Possibly Smart's mill at Ball's Bluff
See History of 15th Bg. Page 56

most optimistic account of Warren's fate that they could manage. He surely saw signs of their defeat there; he would certainly see more in Washington a few days later.

He spent two more days in the area, watching the Southern pickets patrol on horseback across the river, and visiting the men of another heavily engaged unit, the 15th Massachusetts Infantry. This regiment had suffered even worse casualties than Warren's. Thirteen Northborough men who had been members of the Clinton Guards returned from the fiasco at Ball's Bluff, a remarkable figure considering the casualties the regiment had taken, although at least one of them, Henry Kenney, had been wounded. One other townsman who will be mentioned shortly had not returned. From these survivors Eames apparently learned nothing more of Warren, although he acknowledged on November 1 that both the officers and enlistees of the 15th "treated us with marked respect and attention."

On Saturday, November 2 Eames returned to Washington, where he spent some time at the patent office and at the Smithsonian Institute. An inventive man who made carriages, wheel spokes and shoeboxes,[55] he may have had business at the patent office. On Sunday he visited wounded soldiers at Georgetown and in Washington. It is very likely that some Northborough men were there. Ninety-five men from the 15th and 20th Massachusetts regiments were wounded in that bloody day at Ball's Bluff. One was Josiah Proctor of the 20th, who subsequently wrote home to his parents:

> *I was hit with a ball in the back in a heavy crossfire about 4½ o'clock and started down to the River alone. Lieut[enant] Perry assisted me part way down, then gave me into the hands of two soldiers who helped me down to the River where they were carrying wounded soldiers across in boats, but my two helpers left me so I could get no one to help me into a boat until the last boat and I was the last one in it at that. We then started across, the boat tipping every now and then, got across, jumped into the water half my length, crawled up the bank, the bullets coming around us like hail until I got behind a shed on the Island.[56]*

It was on October 27, a week before Columbus Eames visited the hospital, that Proctor had explained his injury and given additional news of Northborough men. Although Eames does not mention Proctor specifically in his diary, he must have received his version of the story. The men he identified were all Northborough enlistees.

Joshua Proctor of the 20th Massachusetts Infantry Regiment wrote home regularly, and the family preserved his accounts carefully.

> *The ball entered my back below my left shoulder and came out below my right. From what we can learn Warren Eames is dead. Two of our company saw him and say his eyes were set and he was gasping his last. Amos* [unidentified] *we can not get track of…I saw Charlie Shaw and Waldo Maynard after I was wounded Monday night. They were all right. They did not* [know] *whether Charles Warren was alive or not…Thomas Burdett is in the hospital taking care of us so I shall not suffer for anything that can be got.*

The following day, November 4, Columbus Eames visited the Capitol dome. With perhaps some exaggeration he claimed, "with a glass I could see the encampments of hundreds of thousands of the United States troops located in Maryland and Virginia." Then he started his return home. "After riding all night in the cars visited the famous New York Park. It was well worth seeing." This would have been the newly constructed Central Park. The following entry marks his return to Northborough on Wednesday evening, November 6: "I am obliged to report that Warren is possibly a wounded prisoner but in all probability he is Dead."

Columbus Eames's diary account goes no further, although his persistence continued. Northborough's best historian to date, Josiah Coleman Kent, tells the rest of the story: "Warren F. Eames was mortally wounded at the battle of Ball's Bluff. One side of his jaw was severely injured; so much so, that it became necessary to remove it by an operation. He survived the operation about two weeks (the exact date of his death is not known), and was buried (without a coffin) at Leesburg, Va."[57]

In May of 1862, as a result of Eames's letter to the postmaster in Leesburg, he received a letter from Susan Luckett, who lived in the town. The wounded Northern soldiers, she told Eames, had been taken to a hospital and cared for.

> *We visited him daily and contributed in various ways to his comfort. You may be assured he did not suffer for anything…Poor fellow, he often tried to talk to us but could not…your son was a stranger in a strange land and our hearts yearned in sympathy over him…if he had recovered he would have been much disfigured…his nose, forehead, eyes and one cheek had sustained no injury…he always looked bright and cheerful and did not seem to suffer one moment's pain…a day or two before his death he looked much better, and when I went into his room (never shall I forget his bright cheerful look) he seemed so glad to see me, and still tried to talk…I trust that this letter may relieve your mind of all anxiety that you may have felt with regard to your son's comfort.*[58]

According to Kent, Eames returned south, recovered his son's body and brought it back to Northborough. But since he had also written that Warren Eames had been buried without a coffin some seven months previously in Leesburg, this appropriation of the body seems unlikely under the circumstances.

On June 11 Elizabeth Allen in Northborough wrote her sister Mary:

> *Today has been the funeral of Warren Eames, who was killed at Ball's Bluff, and whose body has lately been recovered. It was a military funeral, under the direction of the selectmen, and all the ministers took part in it. It seems that he lived a fortnight, and a letter was read, from a lady who with her sister visited him almost every day. They were the only ladies who did visit the hospital, and what they were able to tell of him was a great satisfaction to his friends of course. He was always bright and pleasant, tho' with such a frightful wound.*[59]

The stones for Warren Eames and for some other Civil War soldiers in the Howard Street Cemetery must be cenotaphs. A memorial for all of them was needed, and Columbus Eames, as we shall see, did not rest in his efforts both to honor Warren and those who paid the price of their lives and to assist the living victims of the war.

On that same fatal day at Ball's Bluff, one of the Clinton guards, Thomas N. Woodward Jr. of the 15th Massachusetts Infantry, was one of several hundred other Union men captured. They were taken to Leesburg where they had to endure insults from a crowd of people. Although he was surely wounded, he may have been among the captives who were forced to march sixteen miles to Manassas Junction, arriving on the morning of October 23. That evening the prisoners were loaded on cattle cars. They arrived the following morning at Richmond, the Confederate capital, where they were confined in a brick building that had served as a warehouse and tobacco factory. At some point Woodward was taken to a hospital. There the second Northborough victim of the war died on November 25.[60]

CR&SO

Northborough had been supporting the war effort since April. One day after Lincoln's call for volunteers a warrant was posted in town calling for a town meeting the next day, April 17. At the meeting one citizen pointed out that one day's notice was inadequate to call a town meeting; the actions taken that day might well be invalidated. The gathering became a "citizens' meeting" that urged volunteering, providing for the volunteers and caring for their families. At another meeting a week later the town voted to pay the volunteers one dollar for each day on which they trained and requested a legal town meeting.

This meeting occurred on May 4. Committees were appointed to promote enrollment and provide uniforms and equipment. The dollar-a-day provision was extended to include time in service. On July 4 another town meeting agreed to allow provisions of ten to twenty dollars per month to soldiers' wives and six dollars per month for support of parents or other dependent relatives. The three town selectmen were to administer these payments each month.[61]

The losses at Ball's Bluff sparked an investigation by Massachusetts Governor John Andrew. He sent a committee to Poolesville to investigate the leadership, examine the possibilities of regaining the captured soldiers, or at least send some assistance to them and determine how many replacements would be needed in the decimated regiments. It is likely that the call went forth to a number of Massachusetts towns, and several Northborough men were recruited during the winter and early spring months. Thomas Breach joined the 15th on December 24, Francis Hanley on January 27 and James N. Johnson, Joseph's older brother, on March 31. The only new local member of the 20th at this time was Charles Mayo, at sixteen the youngest of all Northborough enlistees in the war, on February 25.[62]

Otherwise the two armies were encamped for the winter months preparing for the operations of the following year. After Eames and Woodward, there would be no further Northborough fatalities until action began in the spring of 1862. As North and South prepared for military operations the following year, most of the battle scenes remained relatively quiet.

Chapter 4

1862 and Its Bloodiest Day

O ne of the most highly publicized events of the Civil War took place
on March 9, 1862: the battle of the ironclads *Monitor* and *Merrimack*
in Hampton Roads off the Virginia coast. This celebrated battle was less
important than other naval activities, especially the blockades of Southern
ports by Union ships. No native townsmen joined the navy during the Civil
War, but several men who lived in Northborough after the war, Andrew
Falby, David McKenzie, Charles Brigham, William Baird and James
M. Clark, probably took part in this type of action, although details are
lacking.

Not far to the north of Hampton Roads, about a month after the
ironclads clashed, the 15th Massachusetts Regiment, which had spent the
winter at Harper's Ferry after its ordeal at Ball's Bluff, was part of a force
that laid siege to Yorktown. After nearly a month of this watching and
waiting, Charles Shaw wrote to the Reverend Samuel Stanford Ashley in
Northborough on May 3, 1862:

> *Every third day our brigade goes out on picket and is relieved the next*
> *morning. [The] night before last, our company done picket duty. From*
> *my post, it being the outer post, I could see the rebels' pickets and their*
> *fortifications in the daytime. We are posted behind some large trees and keep*
> *a good lookout for them at night. We are advanced as also the rebel pickets*
> *are. I went on my first at seven at night and for four hours lie flat on the*
> *ground with rifle in hand and eyes open ready for anything that should come*
> *along, but saw nothing.*[63]

The men are busy all the time, he adds, building roads on which heavy guns can be brought to bear on the enemy and throwing up fortifications to protect their own batteries. Like other recruits, he contemplates the situation hopefully: "I feel confident that we shall be successful. I hope that the enemy knowing that they must soon yield to the federal forces might surrender, and that peace might be declared and peace and harmony exist where now there is only strife between a once happy and prosperous people."

Shaw and the men were probably wondering whether their impending duty might offer results like those of the famous battle at Yorktown in August of 1781. Could they be on the verge of a battle that might turn the tide against the enemy and move this yearlong struggle toward a glorious end? Might General John Magruder, the commander of the Confederate troops in the town, be forced to replay the role of Lord Cornwallis eighty-one years earlier? After having suffered at Ball's Bluff and then spent several uneventful months in and around Harper's Ferry, was the 15th with its contingent of Northborough men ready to play a positive role?

In an unexpected way, their hopes were denied. The same night that Shaw wrote his letter General John Magruder and his Confederate troops quietly exited the town.[64] The next morning a federal aide-de-camp rode into camp with the news that the fortification was empty. During the month, the Union forces pursued Magruder's army to Fair Oaks, twenty-eight miles to the northwest. There a major battle was fought on May 31 and June 1 with at least two Northborough men wounded. Thomas Breach would return to action later; Francis Hanley, a twenty-eight-year-old farm laborer from Nova Scotia who had settled in Northborough with his wife and fathered two sons, died five weeks after the battle.[65]

The 20th Regiment also fought at Fair Oaks, its men emerging safely. On June 14 Josiah Proctor wrote home to his brother Joseph: "It is hard to think that last year at this time we were all at home together…Whitcomb went down the other day after the mail. He saw Charlie Warren and Larkin…How do you like clicking Sole Leather?…I rec'd a paper from Mr. Ashley about a week ago. Whitcomb got one too."[66] References to Ashley appear constantly in Northborough wartime records. At this point he had led the Evangelical Congregationalists of Northborough for ten years and was clearly considering the possibility of leaving town for full-time duty with the Christian Commission, whose members toured the camps and hospitals "with Bibles and bandages," as they liked to say, or with the American Missionary Association.

Josiah was probably already pondering whether his brother, only nineteen, would follow him into service. On July 26 he sent his parents a letter with this cynical comment: "Now I suppose nearly half of this Army were more or less under the influence of Liquor when they enlisted. I hope Joe won't enlist, but if he does, I hope he will come into the 20 Regt."[67] Sixteen days later that was exactly what his brother did.

One death that summer remains mysterious, as does the man himself. A thirty-six-year-old army surgeon, Albert H. Stacy of the 16th Regiment, was "accidentally killed" at Warrenton Junction, Virginia, on August 27.[68] He had claimed Northborough citizenship as far back as 1848 when he married Mary Ann Bride in Acton, Massachusetts, and he is numbered among the Northborough enlistees of August 1861.[69] Otherwise he can be found in the records of the town in only one intervening year. Stacy was one of two military surgeons from Northborough. His degree of training is also a mystery. One of the most common practices that these men had to perform was the excision of patients' extremities to stave off gangrene, and no doubt Stacy had by the time of his death performed many of these procedures.

⊂ℛℬↄ

With one-year enlistments of the previous year about to expire, that summer Northborough chose to pay one hundred dollars to each volunteer "to the number of seventeen, who shall enlist for three years and be credited to the town." On August 27 the fee was increased to $125 for even a nine-month's volunteer. From July to September there were forty enlistments.[70] Men well into their twenties, thirties and even some in their forties were stepping forward. In October Walter C. Rice, a forty-five-year-old carpenter from Lancaster, enlisted from Northborough.

Women's wartime duties were taken very seriously. On August 3, Reverend Allen noted that a difficulty had grown up after the seventy-two-year-old pastor's assistant, Trowbridge Forbush, had accused the women of Northborough "in no measured terms for their backwardness & lukewarmness in working for the soldiers." One outraged woman arose and "produced a list of all the articles that had been made for the army since the war began." Reverend Allen, who seems to have taken a back seat amidst this uproar, reported a happy ending. In "a patriotic discourse on Sunday" Forbush apologized.[71]

To some of the Allens the war was indeed one over slavery. Thomas Prentiss Allen wrote regularly to his father from New Bedford, Massachusetts, where he was teaching. In April of 1862 he insisted, "the result must be the overthrow of slavery, both because the rebels are too obstinate to yield till the deathblow is struck and because our people have almost unanimously come to demand that as the prospective condition of peace."[72] Another of his themes in his letters to his father was his own sense of his futility. Prentiss, who was forty years old, wrote in August that "it shames me continually to think how little I have done and am doing...And I cannot avoid the reflection that in future years I must look back with shame to the little I was able to do towards settling the great question of the age."[73]

CRSO

One casualty at Fair Oaks—a Southern one—had by this time changed the course of the war. When General J.E. Johnston was seriously wounded, Jefferson Davis immediately replaced him with Robert E. Lee as commander of the northern Virginia army. Lee soon began to outfight and outfox Lincoln's reluctant General George B. McClellan. Instead of defending Richmond, Lee decided to apply pressure toward Washington. On September 4 his men began to cross the Potomac into Maryland. He was hampered in one respect in a way beneficial to the Federal forces who now found themselves often on the defensive. In one of the most famous *faux pas* of the war, someone dropped his orders to his troops on a field where the Confederates had bivouacked. For one part of Lee's plan—the capture of Harper's Ferry—McClellan could now prepare.

Ten miles north of Harper's Ferry stood Sharpsburg, Maryland. Here on September 17, the bloodiest day in American history—not to be outdone even by the events of September 11, 2001—befell both North and South. The 15th and 20th Massachusetts Regiments, seldom far apart throughout the war, were among the vast forces that collided at Antietam Creek near Sharpsburg. (As often happened, the two sides had different names for the same battle. To the Confederates it was the Battle of Sharpsburg; in the North the battle was fought at Antietam.) Over one hundred thousand men are thought to have taken part; an astonishing twenty thousand casualties resulted.

Five Northborough men died from wounds suffered that day. One was John Burke, the only Northborough man known to have deserted, twelve days after his enlistment. But he rejoined and was a member of the 28th Massachusetts Regiment when he fell. No fewer than four men of the hard-pressed 15th were killed or mortally wounded that day.[74] Some of them were most likely slaughtered from the wrong direction. Tiered behind the 15th was an inexperienced New York regiment that began to fire into the backs of their colleagues. Before Second Corps Commander Edwin Sumner could stop them, much damage had been done to a unit that was at the same time facing withering fire from Paul Semmes's brigade of Virginians and Georgians, strongly supported by J.E.B. Stuart's aggressive artillery. Eventually, all the 15th could do was retreat into a wooded area.[75] The four

A gallant 1st Sergeant, Joseph P. Johnson of the 15th Massachusetts Infantry Regiment, died of injuries suffered at Antietam on September 17, 1862.

Waldo Maynard was one of four Northborough members of Company C, 15th Massachusetts Infantry Regiment, to die as a consequence of Antietam.

Charles Warren of Company C, 15th Massachusetts Infantry Regiment, was another Antietam victim.

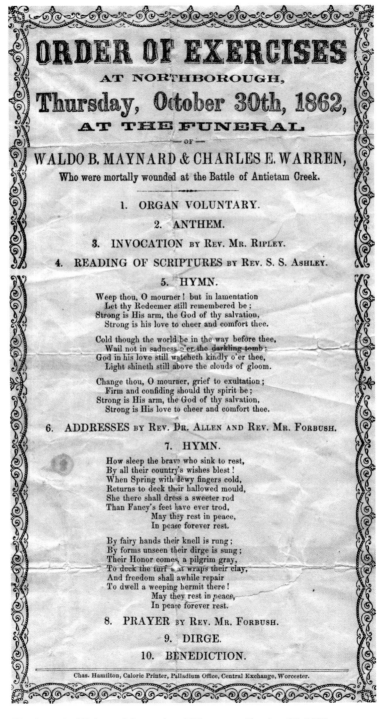

ORDER OF EXERCISES

AT NORTHBOROUGH,

Thursday, October 30th, 1862,

AT THE FUNERAL

— OF —

WALDO B. MAYNARD & CHARLES E. WARREN,

Who were mortally wounded at the Battle of Antietam Creek.

1. ORGAN VOLUNTARY.

2. ANTHEM.

3. INVOCATION BY REV. MR. RIPLEY.

4. READING OF SCRIPTURES BY REV. S. S. ASHLEY.

5. HYMN.

Weep thou, O mourner! but in lamentation
Let thy Redeemer still remembered be;
Strong is His arm, the God of thy salvation,
Strong is his love to cheer and comfort thee.

Cold though the world be in the way before thee,
Wail not in sadness o'er the darkling tomb;
God in his love still watcheth kindly o'er thee,
Light shineth still above the clouds of gloom.

Change thou, O mourner, grief to exultation;
Firm and confiding should thy spirit be;
Strong is His arm, the God of thy salvation,
Strong is His love to cheer and comfort thee.

6. ADDRESSES BY REV. DR. ALLEN AND REV. MR. FORBUSH.

7. HYMN.

How sleep the brave who sink to rest,
By all their country's wishes blest!
When Spring with dewy fingers cold,
Returns to deck their hallowed mould,
She there shall dress a sweeter sod
Than Fancy's feet have ever trod,
    May they rest in peace,
    In peace forever rest.

By fairy hands their knell is rung;
By forms unseen their dirge is sung;
Their Honor comes, a pilgrim gray,
To deck the turf that wraps their clay,
And freedom shall awhile repair
To dwell a weeping hermit there!
    May they rest in peace,
    In peace forever rest.

8. PRAYER BY REV. MR. FORBUSH.

9. DIRGE.

10. BENEDICTION.

Chas. Hamilton, Caloric Printer, Palladium Office, Central Exchange, Worcester.

The funeral of Privates Maynard and Warren on October 30, 1862, was conducted by ministers of all three Northborough Protestant churches.

who died were First Sergeant Joseph P. Johnson, John P. Larkin, Waldo B. Maynard and Charles E. Warren. Overall, Lieutenant General John W. Kimball's 15th suffered 318 casualties—more than half the regiment.

Another man well known in Northborough, having studied in the Allens' boarding school as a boy was Captain Richard Derby. Elizabeth Allen wrote to Mary on September 25:

Our 15th regiment so cut to pieces—every Northboro' man killed, wounded, or missing, and to us the saddest of all, Richard Derby's death. We did not believe it at first, but it had been confirmed before the receipt of Walter Gale's letter last evening. He was killed almost instantly—his body brought at once to Walter…but afterwards they were obliged to leave their dead and fall back, so I fear his mother cannot procure his body. His life has been dear and pleasant to many, but few know what he was at home so well as I. I shall always be glad of the little visit I made there—the house is full of him—little things he had made or collected for the convenience of the older ones, or amusement of the children.[76]

Walter Gale, mentioned in the above letter, was the son of Northborough's richest man, who was known for his early militia experience as Captain Cyrus Gale. The young Gale, who had been studying law, entered the military as a private but was quickly commissioned and would soon be promoted to captain. He took an extraordinary interest in the welfare of his men, especially those from Northborough. His admiration for Derby shines through a letter he wrote to the latter's mother.

We left camp in cheerful spirits, though with something like a premonition that great events were at hand. I chatted pleasantly with Richard, who was almost a brother to me, and we went forward hand in hand, as it were, as we had often done before. When we approached the enemy, he asked me to attend to the men on the right of the company while he gave orders to those on the left. In a moment heavy volleys were poured into our ranks, and finding myself slightly wounded I sought the shelter of a tree. While binding my wound, I saw the lieutenant [Derby was at this time actually a captain] *cheering on his men in the most heroic manner; it was a scene that I never can forget. Two minutes later he also was laid at the foot of the tree, fatally wounded in the temple. He was quite unconscious, apparently in almost a childlike sleep, and thus, without suffering, he passed from life to immortality.*

I had found in him such a genial companion, with so much to love and respect, that I could not quite reconcile myself to the thought that we were

This photograph of Antietam Creek was made after the terrible battle of September 17, 1862.

parted for this life, and yet I almost longed to be with him, if I might leave such a fair name and glorious record. This line is constantly in my mind, and will always associate itself with his memory: 'That life is long which answers life's great end.' [77]

Of the ordeals that Northborough family members endured in the wake of Antietam, Keziah Johnson's was one of the most harrowing, as Elizabeth Allen made clear on October 11:

Joseph Johnson…died a week ago at Washington and it was very sad that his wife was not with him as she might have been if they had not been encouraged by favorable reports…At last they telegraphed for her—he had been wishing to see her, and she went on—but just after she had started came another telegram of his death, and she reached Washington an hour after the body had left for the North…He was a very brave, efficient little fellow, and had to take the command, being sergeant of the Co. after Richard was killed and Walter wounded and received his wound when urging on his men…When his mind was wandering toward the last it was very natural to be upon that—and his last words were "Close up, boys, don't let them break thru." He had done much service, not having lost a day before. [78]

Strangely, it might seem, the battle was considered a victory for the North, despite the comparably heavy losses on both sides. Historians have generally agreed that it ended the Confederacy's hopes of obtaining foreign recognition and reversed the trend of declining morale among Union soldiers. Also, a number of historians have concluded that it provoked Abraham Lincoln's proclamation of emancipation. [79]

In Northborough, the three selectmen issued a "to whom it may concern" letter on September 20: "This may certify that the bearers, Rev. S.S. Ashley and C. Eames, citizens of this town, are on a mission to the recent battle fields in Maryland to look after and care for the wounded and sick of the men from this place who were engaged in the late struggle." [80] These two men were not the only civilians to visit the camps and assist their townsmen, but they obviously were the most prominent.

Those who survived Antietam included the two Proctor brothers, who wrote a joint letter home. Joseph found it "a pretty hard battle I should think. The ball struck me in the back…The first we knew they was right in behind us and [that] is where the ball came from him that hit me and knocked me flat, but it did not go into my back. It burnt and made a sore place, and in about two minutes another hit me but done no hurt." [81] Josiah,

Walter Gale, who enlisted as private and became a major, was intensely loyal to his subordinates in the 15th Massachusetts Infantry Regiment.

who knew all the local victims, at this point had heard only that Warren was wounded and missing and Larkin thought dead. On October 28 he wrote again from Harper's Ferry. Charles Warren, he had heard, "must lose his leg or his life and perhaps both. Levi Whitcomb and Charlie Mayo are well. Joe is well."[82]

On October 2, Josiah told his parents of a great moment in his life: "Uncle Abe arrived at the ferry and reviewed troops and was cheered tremendously. It is the first time I have ever seen him, he looks some as I expected to see him only more pale and careworn."[83] But the saddest news for Mr. and Mrs. Proctor was yet to come. In the Battle of Fredericksburg in December, with Josiah by this time in the hospital, Joseph, only four months after his induction "was shot through the side and crawled off the field and was carried to one of the hospitals in the city. He died there that night…Poor boy, he is gone and I alone am left to you."[84] On the 21st Josiah, whose wounded arm was not healing, wrote that he had heard "that we lost 13,000 men and I can't see that this has accomplished anything. I have got Joseph's knapsack, a shirt, pair of drawers and his pipe and that is all."[85]

On the day after Christmas, Elizabeth Allen wrote to her sister that "Capt. Gale has been very sick all the week, and now has lost his mind after partially recovering it."[86] But Gale recovered, was soon back with the 15th. He would live until 1927, when he died at ninety-three, only one year less than the lifespan of his venerable father back home.[87]

Ten townsmen died in the struggles of 1862; many more were sick and injured. The year was an exceedingly bitter one. Yet one aggrieved woman saw a happier ending. Lizzie Peverley, married before the war with one young son, no doubt already knew what others would read in the *Massachusetts Spy* of October 20. Her husband Horace, one of the Clinton Guard, like hundreds of other combatants at Antietam Creek, was hospitalized in Frederick, Maryland. A twenty-three inch column listed the injuries of just Worcester-area soldiers. The designation of his wounds—"both legs" might have made many readers fear that he had lost them completely, for such surgery was common. But Peverley would return to his career as a painter after the war. Discharged as disabled on February 18, 1863, he became the father of his second son, Harry, the following January. It seems likely that he recovered the use of his legs.

Overall, however, 1862 proved a very difficult year, with ten townsmen dead and many others wounded and sick. Some of the other survivors were surely wondering, like Josiah Proctor, whether what they were enduring was truly worthwhile.

Chapter 5

Gettysburg to Cold Harbor

As the year 1863 began, Northborough women were working to support their warriors. "Last week father and I were invited to a great party at the new hotel, got up by Mrs. Rice, to get money for the Sanitary Commission," Elizabeth Allen wrote to her sister on January 21. "We found it almost entirely a dancing party…As it was the first time I had been out this winter, and I had one good dance, I had a tolerably good time—and father an excellent one. Captains Henry Bailey and Walter Gale were there—the former will return to duty as soon as possible and the latter went Monday morning."[88] A month later, this and another party brought in $75 [close to $1,000 in today's money], and many slippers, bed quilts and other such items were made.[89]

The Sanitary Commission had proven to be a great help to the troops. Although its authorities were men, it grew out of a meeting held only a few days after the outbreak of war by a New York women's group which became the Women's Central Association of Relief. With help from Dr. Henry W. Bellows, pastor of All Souls Unitarian Church in New York, the idea caught on. The new Sanitary Commission would examine such things as diet, clothing, cooks, camping grounds—anything that might help prevent disease among the inexperienced troops. Physicians were employed to inspect camps and suggest to commanders improvements in drainage, cooking procedures and cleanliness and send reports back to the commission. Generally speaking, the inspectors received cooperation from the officers. The collection of supplies was left largely to local branches. One defect of the commission was its failure to acknowledge the work of Clara Barton, whose own assistance to wounded soldiers was carried on independently for the most part.[90]

A nurse of the Sanitary Commission looks after Civil War wounded.

One of the controversies of the war absorbing both North and South was the Union's use of black troops. Authorized by President Lincoln's Emancipation Proclamation, the decision worried many Northerners, but Elizabeth Allen wrote positively to her sister on June 2, 1863, "The departure of the colored regiment from Boston last week you know was a great event. Father saw them and agrees with everybody else that they appeared finely."[91] A few weeks later, when the regiment stormed Fort Wagner in Charleston, South Carolina, its white commander, Colonel Robert Gould Shaw, and nearly half the recruits were dead. The town sent one black man named Richard Overton (his residence went unrecorded; it was not Northborough) to the war, and several townsmen served in units that worked closely with black regiments. As we shall see, a white soldier from the town would later seek a position in a black regiment. A week after this assault, another on the same fort decimated the 24th Massachusetts Regiment, although four Northborough members came through it safely.[92]

Posed here are members of the Sanitary Commission, an organization dedicated to promoting the health of Union soldiers.

Referring to the situation before the war in a letter of July 10, Elizabeth declared to Mary that "Our country never seemed meaner than then, nor nobler than now. We are sure now of righteous souls to save it." But at this time draft riots in New York required a regiment to be brought from Gettysburg to restore order. Elizabeth's sister Lucy was living there, "near enough to be frightened," the family thought.[93] Her youngest brother, William, the man who had observed the tense situation following a Wendell Phillips lecture in Boston in December of 1860, was thirty-three years old, his life having corresponded almost exactly to that of abolitionist William Lloyd Garrison. By this time William, for seven years now a teacher and principal in a classical school near Boston, was inflamed by a compulsion to serve in some capacity. He and his wife of one year decided to go to South Carolina to work for the Freedman's Aid Association. The following year he went to St. Louis, from which he was sent to Helena, Arkansas, for the Sanitary Commission, where he taught African Americans. Returning to South Carolina during the final months of the war, he served as a superintendent in Charleston.[94]

Northborough was learning that war was expensive. The budgets of such towns faced the prospect of bounties and medical examinations for volunteers, the heavy expenses involved in returning the bodies and properties of veterans to town when possible and supporting their funerals, although few bodies of soldiers who fell in battle, and not even all of those who perished in hospitals, were returned to town. These and other military expenses amounted to $4,611.95 by the year 1863, a considerable portion of the town budget.[95]

⊂∂⊱⊰∾

To return briefly to mid-September 1862, when thousands of Northern and Southern men were massing at Antietam, the newly organized 34th Infantry Regiment was settling at Fort Lyon, one of the outposts formed to protect Washington. Company C of the 34th consisted almost entirely of recruits from communities in the Worcester area, seventeen of them from Northborough, most having been sworn in together on July 31. The unit would remain there until the following June. In the fall of 1862 the main problem for this unit was not the armed enemy but disease. Many men suffered from fever, chills, rheumatism and measles. In a letter to a friend, Peter Gamache, one of the Northborough enlistees, commented that six Company C men were in the hospital on March 3 and that thirteen from Company H had been carried there in one day. Of something over one thousand men in the regiment, no fewer than 120 were in the hospital or in quarters. Gamache was also wondering whether Northborough had filled its quota. "I should think that those $700 [bounties] would start some one for I don't think they will have to stay here three years more, half of that time but it is hard telling to be sure."[96]

Probably the next most serious problem was boredom. How did the Northborough men spend evenings in camp? Here is a description by William S. Lincoln, the second ranking officer of the regiment.

> *Look over the camp with me and notice how the men spend their evening hours. Here can be seen a bright eyes, flaxen haired young man, whose education at home this call to arms has interrupted, pursuing by the dim light of the regulation candle the study of his favorite Latin author— while, some few tents removed, by the glimmer of a like dip, a group of more thoughtless comrades are deep in the mysteries of old sledge or euchre. Withdrawn to a remote corner of the camp, a party of earnest and devoted*

ones join in devout supplication for grace and support in the trying scenes which may lie before them, while others, more self-reliant, indulge in comments upon the latest movements of the army, or growl about the order just issued from Regimental Headquarters. The smothered voice of some home-sick volunteer, asking in broke notes "Do they miss me at home," is fairly drowned by the thundering chorus of a party of rollicking ones who leave "John Brown's body mouldering in the grave, as they go marching on."[97]

The men would wind up spending almost as much time in this place that John Brown had already made famous as they spent in Fort Lyon. By the time they arrived there in mid-July 1863, one of the sick Northborough men, eighteen-year-old Perry W. Towle, had died in a hospital in Washington.[98] While there they met with another regiment well populated with Northborough- and Worcester-area men, the 51st, which spent only a few days at this militarily significant confluence of the Potomac and Shenandoah Rivers. So a number of soldiers were able to renew friendships.[99]

At this point neither of these units had done anything remarkable. Life would get much more difficult for the 34th, but an account of the 51st, which was formed in September of 1862 and remained in existence for less than a year, exemplifies another aspect of military life. Only the 15th and the 34th would have more Northborough men than the 51st. Eleven of them found themselves together in Company A, whose commander, Captain Edwin A. Wood of Worcester, wrote a short history of the company. This company was part of a regiment clearly not designated for combat duty. If the ages of the Northborough members are taken as even roughly characteristic of the men in the 51st, it was a relatively old group, eight of the Northborough men being twenty-nine or over, the oldest, William B. Babcock, forty-one. Like most of these older men, he was married with children. His fourth child would be born while he was away.[100] There were some younger members, including Cyrus H. Mentzer, only eighteen, whose relative George Mentzer had enlisted in the 24th Regiment a year earlier.

The duties of Captain Wood's company consisted largely of building and destroying: constructing corduroy roads and ditches to assist Union combatants and burning bridges and tearing up tracks near New Bern, North Carolina, to forestall advances by the enemy. At one point they were moved to Baltimore to "search through the city for the purpose of securing such arms as might be found secreted or in the possession of improper persons."[101]

Not a single man from the whole regiment was listed as having been killed in action, and Company A was only fired upon briefly, but the nature

Cyrus H. Mentzer of the 51st Massachusetts Infantry Regiment in later life.

of their work still put lives in danger. Much of their labor was in swampy land, and forty-four men died of disease, including several from Company A, but all of the Northborough men from this workaday regiment returned safely.

The great battles of 1863 included Chancellorsville, Vicksburg on the western front, and Gettysburg. One Northborough-born man, Joseph A. Davis, a nineteen-year-old lieutenant who had moved to New York and

George Mentzer enlisted in the 24th Massachusetts Infantry Regiment.

served in its 149th Regiment, wrote to "Sat," apparently a friend, on April 14, before Chancellorsville.

> *The Lord grant that we may succeed, but Oh! At what a cost! For many must fall, and how many poor hearts will bleed for lost sons, husbands, fathers, and lovers. Who knows but that I may be among the honored ones who fall in defense of their loved country; and if it be so, then may I meet*

Joseph A. Davis was born in Northborough but was serving in a New York regiment at Chancellorsville when he met his death.

my fate with the calmness in which I speak of it now to you. I have not, as I have often told you before, the least idea that I shall survive a great battle, for it is mine to fall, I most seriously believe, and so be it.[102]

Chancellorsville became another victory for the outmanned but brilliant General Lee, and Davis fell as he honorably but gloomily supposed he would.

The 36th Massachusetts Infantry, including Captain Henry Bailey and Austin Dandurand, fought at Vicksburg. Capturing this town at a crucial point on the Mississippi River with its connecting rail line sundered Southern forces east and west of the river. At Baton Rouge another local enlistee, John Breach of the 38th Regiment, died on May 11.[103] But most of the Northborough men were in the east, where one of the great battles would be fought that summer.

This battle, in time the generator of the most famous American address, was an almost accidental encounter. For various reasons—which did not include any prospect of overrunning Northern territory—General Robert E. Lee decided to plunge through the narrow ten or twelve miles of western Maryland into Pennsylvania in June. Meanwhile the Union army, ordered to protect Washington, also marched northward, bent on staying between the Confederates and the nation's capital. In the streets of Gettysburg on July 1, some idling troops of both sides discovered each other. These matters reported, the two armies fell back, gathered reinforcements, and the next day the Battle of Gettysburg began.

Among those present and wounded was Walter Gale of the 15th Massachusetts, which marched to a position behind Cemetery Ridge before dawn on July 2. In the afternoon the Confederates began firing, and the 15th was ordered to a position well in front of the line of Union troops. Near dusk, with the 15th attempting to install a barricade of rails, the Confederates attacked, and the 15th found itself being shot at from front and rear. Much of the Union shot fell short, and some of the heavy fatalities the regiment took came from their own side. Three officers and nineteen enlisted men were killed.[104]

Josiah Proctor was also present. The 20th Regiment had begun marching northward in mid-June during a heat wave. On June 29, he wrote his parents that they were halted "near Fredericksburg," a slip, for his unit was eighty miles north of that city in Frederick, Maryland. The regiment continued for another thirty miles, and became one of the numerous military units in the great but indecisive battle that cost the two sides about fifty thousand casualties. On July 5 he wrote again: "We have been in another heavy fight and as usual we have lost heavy." Despite the losses at Gettysburg, Proctor knew that the outcome this time was not one of the defeats to which the valiant men of the 20th had become so accustomed: 'I have got a pretty severe wound in the left forearm. It is not a dangerous wound…The Regt went in with 334 guns and now musters between 90 and 100…We are in the woods and as comfortable as we can be made at present…We have given the Rebs a good thrashing."[105]

Proctor eventually learned that he would not lose his arm but that damage was indeed severe, and he spent most of the rest of his enlistment in hospitals. He later wrote his parents that his arm was "not much better than a wooden one…The inner bone is in two parts and it is all healed up so it can never grow together again."[106] Without him, his regiment would go on to the bloody encounters in the Wilderness, at Spotsylvania, Cold Harbor and Petersburg. Along the way at least ninety-nine regimental members were captured.

CR80

Action for most soldiers did not begin in 1864 until May, but soon many of the men who had enlisted in 1861 would be discharged. On June 28, the town surveyed "Persons Liable to Enrollment in Northborough." There were 237 names of men between eighteen and forty-four—including those already in the service, some of whom would re-enlist. Their occupations were also listed, as well as "causes for exception," if any. Relatively few causes were listed, "defective teeth," "weak lungs" and "consumptive" among them.[107] Most of the men were thus eligible and during the year forty-eight enlisted, most of them from July to October, a list that comes close to matching, month-by-month, the 1861 enlistments. Several non-combatants from the town were assisting at various locations for the Sanitary Commission.

Another development of 1864 was what Massachusetts Governor John Andrew called a "disastrous" aggravation of the disproportion between men and women. He is quoted in the *Report of the School Committee of the Town of Northborough* for the year 1864–65 thus: "It disorders the market for labor; it reduces women and men to an unnatural competition for employments fitted for men alone, tends to increase the number of men unable to support families, and of women who must maintain themselves unaided." In Northborough it provided more jobs for women teachers, as fewer male college students were available for the town's district schools.

CR80

By the spring of 1864, President Lincoln was a glum man. After three years of war, with victory still receding in the distance, he turned to Ulysses S. Grant, who had won impressive victories in the west, to lead the charge against Lee in Virginia. After assessing the situation in the eastern part of the state, Grant hoped to move his army to the right and rear of Lee's at Spotsylvania Court House. After a few hours of light fire, moving the wounded and throwing a light cover of earth over the bodies of the slain, the Army of the Potomac set out after dark on May 7 for Spotsylvania. Lee was determined to hold the Court House, and both armies began marching by different but parallel routes to the town. From the eighth to the twelfth, the two armies fought again, much of the time in the rain, but after repeated Federal assaults and repulses, Lee's troops still held the Court House. Again, the losses were heavy, among them one of Elizabeth Allen's friends. She learned that Captain Henry Bailey of the 36th Regiment, back in Virginia after its role at Vicksburg, had been shot in the head on the final day of the Spotsylvania action and died instantly.

Grant's army continued to press forward. Late in May they crossed the Pamunkey River and approached Cold Harbor. Unlike McClellan—whom Lincoln could never wean from his cautious avoidance of military battles but now was assaulting Lincoln politically as his Democratic opponent in the 1864 election—Grant was an aggressive general, even at the price of heavy casualties. Cold Harbor proved to be the most disastrous of his offensives.

Several regiments with substantial numbers of Northborough men were involved, including the 25th Infantry, which at this point was part of the Eighteenth Corps, specifically in the Second Division commanded by Brigadier General John H. Martindale. At dawn on June 3, Martindale's division, at the center of a line of five Union corps several miles long attacking Lee's men from the east, was selected to lead the assault. Harvey Clark of Gardner, Massachusetts, wrote of the experience: "We started with a yell…The first we saw was a line of men shoulder to shoulder waist high above their works, then a solid sheet of fire, and such a shower of shell and bullets. It is hard to describe the sensation I had. It was like being alone in the midst of a whirlwind."[108]

The offensive stalled, and the toll was a heavy one, particularly for the 25th. George F. Merriam of Company C was killed on the battlefield; Leander Fay of Company G died two days later of his wounds.[109] Two other Company C men who had served in the unit since September of 1861 were wounded, forty-three-year-old Frederick Bartlett in the foot and thirty-one-year-old Alonzo K. Bucklin in both a leg and an arm. J. Waldo Denny, the historian of the unit, claimed that 220 of the 300 men of the 25th who participated at Cold Harbor were killed, wounded or lost.[110] In this battle, of which a Confederate general remarked, "It was not war, it was murder," the 25th suffered as badly as any unit of Northborough soldiers. Of nine remaining men who had joined in Northborough at about the same time, only two escaped death or injury. Four were disabled. The major battle was over after June 3, although skirmishing went on until June 12. The only two Northborough men alive and unwounded would have heard, on June 5, a band in the Confederate camp playing *Dixie*. Yes, there was a band, and an answering Union one, which offered *The Star-Spangled Banner* and *Yankee*

George F. Merriam had served for nearly three years in the 25th Massachusetts Infantry Regiment when he was killed in June of 1864.

Doodle. Each side, Harvey Clark reports, cheered its own band.[111] After Cold Harbor, the Union army moved on to Petersburg, which involved the efforts of many Northborough men.

Here must be introduced an infantry regiment not formed until April of 1864, but baptized with fire early. The unit owed its existence to a remarkable man who attracted several hardy Northborough area men, among them two of the few who had served in the Louisiana campaign. The 57th Massachusetts Regiment was formed at Worcester, Massachusetts, by Colonel William F. Bartlett. This indomitable man had lost a leg at Yorktown, Virginia, in 1862, been assigned to the 49th Regiment in November of that year, been wounded again at Port Hudson, Louisiana, and mustered out in September of 1863.[112]

Francis Moore Harrington of Boylston, Massachusetts, joined Colonel Bartlett's new regiment on March 19, 1864. Harrington had enlisted in the 53rd at its organization on October 17, 1862, and early the next year was shipped to Louisiana. Having seen some action at Port Hudson on the Mississippi, he, like many of the Northern men, found the climate difficult. In his diary he complained chiefly of diarrhea, but the doctors put him on camphor and opium pills (three times a day, Harrington reported). Ill health put more than four times as many of his colleagues out of action than did combat. In this respect the 53rd resembled the 51st. In his prior ten months' service Harrington had not been cast into much military danger; now he would be.[113]

Harrington always kept a diary; therefore, the story of the 57th will begin with him. Although not originally listed as a Northborough enlistee, Harrington was later so designated, probably because his parents lived in Northborough. He received a bounty of $727 from federal, state, and local sources for his latest display of fervor and would make his home permanently in Northborough; now he was part of a regiment traveling by train and ship to Philadelphia, Baltimore and Annapolis.[114]

Then, as became foot soldiers, the 57th marched to Washington, most of the men on two legs, but Colonel Bartlett on one sound one and one of cork. As part of General Ambrose Burnside's Ninth Corps, Harrington's regiment passed before President Lincoln, watching from the balcony of Willard's Hotel, on April 25. The House and Senate both adjourned to watch the review also. Two days later, while bivouacked at Alexandria, Harrington, probably remembering his months in the Deep South, "threw away my Overcoat this morn."

Harrington's diary requires a measure of reading between the lines. He describes his part in dangerous battles briefly and vaguely, saying, for instance, that he "worked hard." He often tells more about the amenities of life—if, for example, he had a chance to take a shower. For a few days in late April and early May the 57th marched south. On May 3 at Rappahannock Station the company was drilled in "target practice" and in "loading and firing," suggesting that the unit was barely trained only two days before the famous Battle of the Wilderness.

On May 4, after a short morning march, the unit "loafed until 5 P.M. then marched until 2 A.M.," at which point Harrington and another soldier "fell out." Sometimes falling out meant quitting, but these two men struggled for hours seeking their unit. Today one sails through that portion of Interstate 95 connecting Washington and Richmond in a few minutes. To the regimental historian, the Wilderness consisted of "deep jungles and dark ravines…It did not possess one cheerful feature and seemed the last place in the world for the habitation of man."[115]

Harrington and his companion missed the first day of the battle. The men had to report to Generals Meade and Burnside; if they were punished in any way for their absence, Harrington does not report it. The next day his Company K spent with the baggage train, but the experience proved more onerous than guard duty. Their regiment was broken in the conflict, but a group of men including Harrington "rallied around the flag and [were] going through heated times." Harrington seldom gets very specific about such incidents. John Anderson, member and future historian, describes the incident as follows:

> *The regiment had been assailed from the flank as well as the front, and in falling back the colors had been seen so near the enemy, and then lost to sight, that it was believed they had been captured; but at this critical point, Lieutenant-Colonel Chandler, who commanded the regiment, Colonel Bartlett having been wounded, ordered the men who were near the colors to lie down and conceal them. They had hardly obeyed this order when the enemy charged down the plank road near them, and, for a time, they were surrounded, but in the general confusion they were evidently overlooked… Their escape was due to their own gallantry and the dense thicket which partially concealed them.*[116]

Anderson goes on for several pages about this near crisis and concludes: "Colors are as important to a regiment as the head to a man or war paint to an Indian."[117] Truly, these days—Thursday, May 5 through Saturday, May 7—were Harrington's and the regiment's baptism of fire.

The Army of the Potomac, over one hundred thousand men, had fought to a draw against an outmanned but formidably entrenched opponent. At the end both armies held the same ground. Over four thousand bodies lay on the broken landscape; the wounded and missing of the two sides ran to about 24,000. No fewer than 252 men of the 57th Regiment were killed, wounded or missing. Anderson, confirming the number long afterwards when the losses had been meticulously counted, observed that "many of the wounded died soon after the battle, and many of the missing died in Confederate prisons. Very few ever returned to duty again."[118]

On Sunday, May 8, Harrington wrote that the men "were relieved last night before dark [and] had a scare just after dark," which he never describes at all! Unlike Proctor, who would supply his parents with grim details, and many other soldiers who wrote diaries, Harrington, writing as it seems to himself, seems unwilling to delve into the horrors. Perhaps they were so deeply ingrained in him that he did not need to; his brief references were probably all he needed to recall them to mind. The scare must have taken place while the Union force was withdrawing from the Wilderness and throwing up defenses at Spotsylvania Court House. Even Anderson here is not very specific: "The two long days of darkness and horrors through which we had passed seemed a lifetime."[119]

The 57th marched off on Sunday and by Monday were supporting a Maine battery at Spotsylvania, where Harrington worked at "throwing up earthworks." Although the toll at Spotsylvania and at the Spotsylvania Court House over the next two weeks was heavy, Harrington's regiment suffered much less than in the Wilderness. A dozen townsmen served in the 57th. One, nineteen-year-old Lorenzo Fletcher, died on May 10, perhaps from disease, perhaps from action in the Wilderness or at Spotsylvania; the records do not tell us. The rest continued, but except for Harrington's diary and a few letters from Guilford P. Heath, individual records of the other men have not come to light. At North Anna River late in May, Harrington reports that "Our Noble & Brave Lt. Col. [Charles L. Chandler] was wounded and left." He died in enemy hands.

The rest of the severely depleted regiment suffered few of the many Union losses at Cold Harbor, but by the middle of June, Harrington, Heath and the other townsmen in the 57th were outside of Petersburg, where for them the action would reach another peak.

Chapter 6

Petersburg to Appomattox

As many as eleven townsmen were marching with the 57th Regiment out of Cold Harbor after dark on June 12, 1864. They were Caleb Austin, Adelbert Bemis (probably), Ezra Bemis, Henry Goulding, Guilford Heath, Edward Lowell, John Palmer, Charles Trowbridge, Gustavus Richardson, Henry Sargent and diarist Francis Harrington. At some point in the next few weeks the Confederates captured Adelbert Bemis. On the 14th the rest of the men arrived at Charles City Court House on the James River. How did these soldiers, most of them relatively recent recruits who had begun the year at home, look? The regimental historian, John Anderson, then one of its lieutenants, described the unit's arrival thus:

> *For the previous six weeks it had been literally fighting by day and marching by night, with very little time for sleep or refreshment. Officers had not been able to obtain a change of clothing, as there could be no delay for the regimental wagons to come up. They were so covered and begrimed with dust and dirt that they would have been disgusted and ashamed of themselves in any other place or position, yet they wore this evidence of hard service, as a distinctive mark of honor earned in the field in defense of their country. Going to war possesses a romantic charm before experience has been gained, but when it comes to hard marching and fighting, with only the coarsest food to eat, and standing guard all night, perhaps through a drenching rain, with blistered feet, tired limbs and aching bones, where it is a crime, punishable with death, to fall asleep; then to fight or march all the next day, rather tarnishes the glamour of war and makes it more realistic; but this is what these men did day after day.*[120]

Guilford Heath wrote home somewhat too optimistically about the welfare of Northborough men in 1864.

As the men marched, they sang, "We'll hang Jeff Davis to a sour-apple tree."[121] The 57th was allowed little respite. Now they had to trek to Petersburg, where vast Union forces were grouping. The regiment was at this stage attached to the 1st Brigade of the 1st Division in the Ninth Army Corps.

Before their recent spurt of activity in the Wilderness, Spotsylvania and across three Virginia streams—the North Anna, Pamunkey and Totopotomoy (the first heavily defended)—three of the Northborough men, Trowbridge, Harrington and Heath, had served in other units. For the others, these few weeks proved a literal baptism of fire. On June 19, Heath found time to write a letter home. He was well, "And so are all of the Northboro boys except Gus Richardson who is feeling a little indisposed, though I think he will be well in a day or two."[122] About Richardson, Heath was apparently wrong, for on July 25 he died in Philadelphia.

The men kicked off again on the night of June 16, "nearly thirty miles without resting," then were allowed to rest until 2:00 p.m. Heath's letter continues:

> The 2nd corps which was in front fighting while we rested had been successful in taking nearly all of the first line of entrenchments but about noon were repulsed in trying to take a very strong position and we were ordered up to try our luck. Our brigade was drawn up in the front line and within about one eighth of a mile of the rebs. Here we lay down partly covered from their fire by a little rise of ground in front though their battery had a fine range on us. We remained in this position waiting for the rest of the corps to come up until nearly sundown when the order came to charge and we went forward double quick through an open corn field, and amidst a shower of shot and shell, and a perfect storm of bullets from the enemy, our boys fel[l] in heaps but still we pushed forward. When within ten rods of the main works we came upon a line of rifle pits where we captured about two hundred sharpshooters. We continued on and over the entrenchments driving the rebs out in such haste that they left their haversacks behind them which were pretty well filled with corncakes. Then we made a mistake by not following them up, had we continued on after them we could easily have captured their battery.

The Corps may perhaps be forgiven for proceeding no further after a night of marching, but finding no one in pursuit, the Confederates soon rallied and returned to try to recapture what they had lost, although the Union prevailed in this struggle:

We now had a pretty tuff fight the mussles of our guns almost touching each other some times when we fired. Still the fight continued sometimes they driving us and then we driving them until about midnight when the rebs retired leaving us in full position of the ground. Here we remained until morning when the 4th Corps came up and took the front and they are still fighting and have drove the rebs about two miles further on.

Francis Harrington had his most dangerous moments in the long siege some weeks later on the night of July 17, which he set forth in his diary in his characteristically laconic way: "Went to the front line of works last night and laid under mortar firing but moved to the rear during the forenoon." We can gauge the intensity of this effort more justly from Anderson's account in his regimental history:

Late on the night of the 17th General Meade ordered an assault upon the enemy's works at four o'clock A.M. of the 18th, by the Second, Fifth and Ninth Corps. The troops moved forward promptly at the designated hour, a large proportion of the fighting again falling upon the Ninth [and thus again on the 57th Regiment]. *As the advance was made the enemy hastily abandoned the intrenchments that had been captured, the previous night, by the First Division of the Ninth Corps, leaving their dead and many of their wounded to fall into our hands. At the angle where the battery was located, of which previous mention has been made, the trenches were found filled with Confederate dead, while the surrounding ground was thickly covered with them. Looking back at the cornfield over which the charges had been made the previous day, it was found thickly strewn with the Federal dead, while the field of corn, which so recently had shown a peaceful husbandry, was now trampled into the bloody ground. Everything showed how desperate the engagement had been.*[123]

Meanwhile, a daring mine project was well under way. To lay a mine under a salient of the high Confederate position, men from General Burnside's Ninth Corps had to try to dig their way secretly for five hundred feet. The operation continued for a month, and the miners laid eight thousand pounds of powder beneath the salient. After the blast was generated, the Corps would storm the fort. A division of black troops would lead, presumably because they had suffered less in battle and were eager to demonstrate their valor. This decision generated a dispute between General Meade, who was second in command to Grant, and Ninth Corps Commander Burnside, either because the generals were sensitive to the criticism that might be made about "shoving these people ahead to get

Francis M. Harrington endured the 1864 Petersburg mine incident and months in a Southern prison.

killed,"[124] as Meade put it, or because neither Meade nor Burnside had full confidence in the effectiveness of the blacks. Burnside's order canceled the plan of having the black troops lead, but they would immediately follow the first division into the fort.

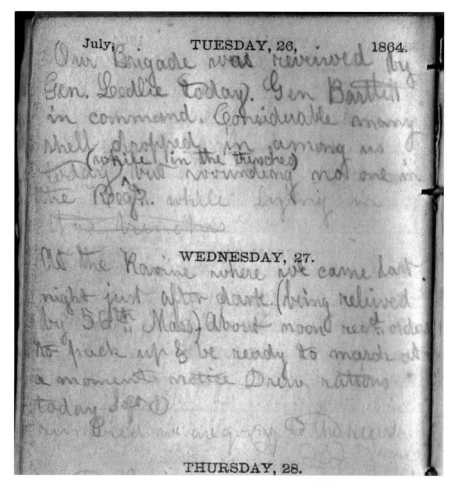

This portion of the diary that Harrington carried through his tour with the 57th Massachusetts Infantry Regiment comes just before his capture.

The commander of the brigade containing the 57th at this point was a man the unit knew well: its originator, William F. Bartlett, now a brigadier general. Mustered out of service the preceding September and eligible, if anybody ever was, to leave the rest of the fighting to others, the one-legged hero had returned for more action.[125]

The First Division of the Ninth Corps, including the 57th, was chosen to lead the charge into the stockade, once the powder had exploded. This was the most precarious part of Francis Harrington's military experience. As usual, his own account of the deed, dated July 30, while accurate, is both moderate and modest. He seems to have written it the following day:

Moved some to the left (last night) opposite the fort which was blown up just at daylight when the 9 A.C. or most of it charged and occupied the works. The Colored troops followed up, the enemy concentrating drove us into the fort again which Gen Bartlett surrendered about Four P.M. when we were marched about 2 miles to the rear under guard.

Here is a bit of Anderson's narrative of the blast:

Suddenly there came a heavy rumble that made the ground tremble, followed by a deep boom; quickly jumping to our feet we saw a black mountain of earth and smoke rising, carrying cannon, caissons, camp equipage and human bodies in one confused mass, about two hundred feet in the air, where it poised for a second, and as it settled back, looked as if it would bury the troops which were formed for the charge.[126]

What Harrington experienced and other Northborough men saw, but would not have been able to articulate as Anderson did, was a "spectacle of appalling grandeur," a scene of destruction and mangled bodies that seemed to paralyze the men who were ordered forward.

The place where this frowning fort once stood was now converted into a huge crater about one hundred and sixty feet long, sixty wide and about twenty-five deep, and looked like the mouth of a volcano, with the cloud of smoke and dust hanging over it.

For the time being the instincts of humanity were the first consideration, and another delay was made while the unfortunate victims were being rescued from living graves.[127]

Among those to be rescued was "our gallant brigade commander, General Bartlett [who] had his artificial leg crushed early in the engagement and was now lying back in the crater as helpless as the buried Confederates around him."[128] What the Northborough men, except the captured Harrington, were experiencing Anderson described Homerically:

The First Brigade, under Colonel Sigfried, made a most gallant attack. The 43rd U.S. Colored Troops attacked the intrenchments, capturing about two hundred prisoners, a stand of colors and recapturing a stand of the National colors that had been lost by a white regiment. The Second Brigade (colored), under Colonel Thomas, was considerably broken in getting through, and only fragments of it were led to the attack, which, after suffering a heavy loss, were driven back and eventually took refuge in the crater, which seemed like a mighty whirlpool, whose suction drew in and engulfed all who came near it, although there was no music of sirens to entice them to meet their doom, or council of Circe to guide them beyond.[129]

Anderson required nearly two pages to list the regimental casualties, noting that many of the twenty-seven missing men were surely among the dead. The Union forces as a whole had been diminished by 4,400 during the Petersburg mine episode.[130]

At this event the 25th Regiment, placed toward the rear, did not suffer. Harvey Clark, the Gardner, Massachusetts member quoted in the last chapter, reported that on August 1 "some of the men went to the front and talked with enemy soldiers," presumably while the bodies were being cleared. In the course of the war, these conferences were not uncommon. The men you did not kill one day you could talk with on another.[131] Already on July 31, Harrington and the captured Union men had been marched away. Wondering where they would be taken, the men heard a guard say "Georgia." This most likely meant Andersonville, whose appalling reputation was well known by this time. One of the three captured Company K men, Stephen H. Phelps of Marlborough, Massachusetts, wound up there, either then or later, and died on August 26. Death records at Andersonville were maintained carefully.[132]

Harrington and the other captured Company K man were luckier. They went to Danville, where they were given "plenty of Corn Bread and bacon & Rice soup" the first night. For most of August he made no entries in his diary; on August 29 he wrote, "The names of the sick and wounded confined in this Prison were taken for Parole this afternoon. Weather Pleasant and a good breeze all day." The next day's entry, though extremely incomplete, is important: "The sick and wounded in all the Prisons and Hospitals in this place were sent off to[ni]ght, serg't Geo H. Parks Co A Regt among the rest. He promised to write to Father for me. [We] were searched for valuables today Weather Pleasant." Harrington does not number himself among the sick and wounded, but he clearly was. Sergeant Parks, a buddy from Milford, Massachusetts, was hoping to be among those exchanged. Harrington's name was announced, but not that of Parks. Seeing the disappointment in Parks's eyes, Harrington stepped aside, and let the man have his place. Sadly, Parks never reached home, dying on September 19 at Annapolis.[133]

Harrington's short daily entries are often about the food. Pea soup was a staple, but as time went on the quality and quantity lessened, for the whole Confederacy was beginning to starve by the early months of 1865. Harrington was destined to be one of the surviving prisoners.

Gustavus Richardson of the 57th Massachusetts Infantry Regiment was one of many Civil War veterans to die of illness.

George A. Prouty of the 34th Massachusetts Infantry Regiment was one of many soldiers to die in the campaigns of the spring and summer of 1864.

To return to another aspect of the war, we left the 34th Regiment in Harper's Ferry; they served there and in the adjoining area until early 1864. Their major adventures came upon their attachment to the 1st Infantry Division, West Virginia, especially in its 1st Brigade from June to Christmas Day of 1864. The battles in which they fought—Lynchburg, Berryville, Winchester, Cedar Creek, Bermuda Hundred—are less well known than some already described, but during this period at least five Northborough enlistees died or earned death wounds. Joseph Dudley, wounded near Staunton on March 31, died on September 4; Corporal George Prouty was fatally wounded at Mount Crawford on June 5; Sergeant Nathaniel Hodgkins died of wounds on September 27; Edwin W. Pierce, wounded at Cedar Creek on October 13, died the day after Christmas; and Sergeant John W. Forbes died a prisoner at Salisbury, North Carolina, on January 13. Finally, Albert H. Carruth died at Alexandria on April 19, ten days after Lee's surrender.[134]

A more fortunate townsman in the 34th, Frank T. Leach, was a line officer who displayed outstanding leadership qualities. When a Confederate force

Captain Frank T. Leach was one of Northborough's most notable leaders. He served as commander of the 34th Regiment and was named to a committee formed to examine officers for regular army duty.

attempted to cross the Shenandoah in August, Leach, with Companies A and G, was sent to resist them. The following January he was sent with a hundred men and five days' worth of rations to scout southward in Loudon County. In April, Leach was given leave to appear before the Examining Board in Washington to apply for a position with a black regiment. Black units were commanded by white men, and Leach obviously saw an opportunity for advancement in such a setting. The application was denied, but he continued to be given forward assignments with the 34th.[135]

From July to September the regiment took part in General Sheridan's Shenandoah Valley campaign, and by December, amidst deaths and disabilities of major officers, Leach was made commander of the regiment, an unusual position for a captain.[136] He proved his leadership on April 1 when the regiment faced an earthwork outside Richmond called Battery Gregg. Lincoln quotes Leach's own account of this action:

> *"When within one hundred yards of the work,"* writes Capt. Leach, our gallant leader on that day, *"we were obliged to lie down, and crawl upon*

our hands and knees; the enemy, all the time pouring grape and canister into our ranks, at a furious rate. But not a man flinched, although dead and dying comrades were lying thickly strewed upon the ground. The ditch around the fort was reached at last, and although the water in it stood waist deep, the brave fellows hesitated not to jump in, and scramble up the bank of the fort, vainly attempting to rush in en masse, and end the bloody struggle. Soon the stars and stripes could be seen floating by the side of the Rebel rag; cheer after cheer rent the air,—the Rebels fighting with the desperation of madmen and shouting to each other 'never surrender! never surrender!' For twenty-seven minutes we hung upon the works, knowing we could not retreat if we wished to. One more rush and we were inside the fort, and for a minute or two there was a hand to hand contest. The works were ours; and the garrison,—dead and alive. Not a man escaped…Very soon the other forts were abandoned by their, or captured by our men. Considering the work we of the 34th had done, our loss was light: being only three officers slightly wounded—five men killed and thirty-two wounded. Arms were stacked, and the men put to work upon a new line of entrenchments, that we might hold what we had gained."[137]

After Lee's surrender, Leach's temporary command ended, but one more honor came to him. Early in June he was the junior officer named to an examining board that would report on the quality of volunteer officers who wished to remain in the service. These men, however, would not include Leach himself, for this brave townsman was mustered out on June 16, 1865.[138]

One of the most melancholy episodes of the war for the families of thousands of Union veterans, including three from Northborough, was the extent of casualties at Andersonville. Until recently, when writers have striven to be more objective, Andersonville was seldom described apart from attempts to cast blame or defend its practices. Had the authorities been the most benevolent of men, they could not have made the place anything but a disaster. It was located in a deforested place; thus, there was little or no wood to cook meals or provide heat in the winter. The prison lacked an adequate water supply, drainage or the capacity to dispose of wastes. By 1864 food was scarce. The Confederacy claimed that the prisoners ate the same food that its own soldiers did, but for the prisoners the pork was uncooked, the cornmeal ground up along with cob and shucks. Thirteen thousand prisoners died from wounds and disease.[139]

One Northborough man, Thomas B. Davis of the 1st Cavalry Division, died there on May 31, 1864. Another, Adelbert W. Bemis, a young farmer from the 57th Regiment, passed away on September 11. Bemis was the second child and oldest boy of the ten children of Elijah and Julia. Bemis

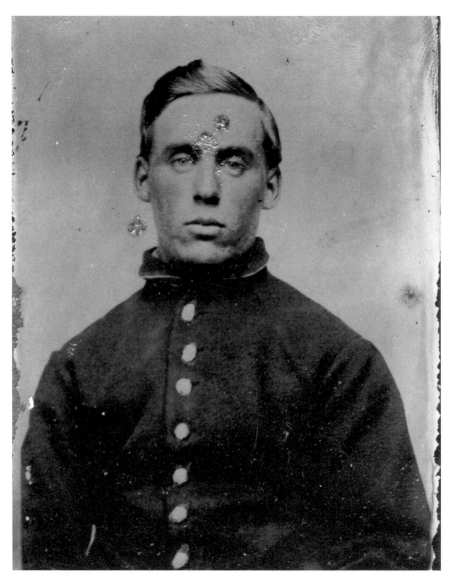

Adelbert Bemis of the 57th Massachusetts Infantry Regiment was one of three Northborough soldiers to die in the infamous prison at Andersonville, Georgia.

lingered in the infamous prison when its population far outran its supposed capacity.[140] Opened in February of that year, the eighteen-acre facility took on as many as thirty-three thousand men by August. The inmates buried their own members, sometimes hundreds in a day, shoulder to shoulder, as many visitors to the graveyard with its vast rows of closely stacked uniform gravestones can attest.[141]

About the time of Bemis's death, an effort to transfer some of the men began, and by the end of November the population had decreased to 1,379. One of them was Charles Shaw of the 20th Regiment, who had written to Reverend Ashley about the upcoming Yorktown battle that never materialized, and who was often mentioned in Josiah Proctor's letters. Shaw had entered the service a month before Proctor. He had survived Ball's Bluff, Antietam, Gettysburg and Cold Harbor, among other battles. His three-year enlistment would have ended in July, but on June 22 he was taken prisoner near Petersburg. He lived longer—which is to say more miserably—than Bemis at Andersonville. Many of the prisoners had been taken to another prison at Thomasville, but Union cavalry raids near that facility forced many back to Andersonville. On Christmas Eve 3,500 prisoners, who had earlier been transferred from this worst of all Southern prisons, were returned. Shaw did not live to see the event; he perished on December 19. Thirteen thousand Union soldiers died there; no one knows how many of the sick and emaciated survivors, the last of whom left in May of 1865, died thereafter from the effects of the experience.[142]

The men outside Petersburg maintained their vigil long after the mine explosion. Several townsmen were involved. Levi Whitcomb, a member of the 20th often mentioned by Josiah Proctor as having endured "hard times" at Gettysburg and earlier, was involved in the struggle at the Weldon Railroad near Petersburg a few weeks after the mine episode. Captured there by the Confederates, Whitcomb had to survive five months as a prisoner. Another Northborough man with a memorable experience on the Weldon was Walter Valentine of the 14th Battery, Light Artillery, who found that the retreating enemy had set their ammunition on fire. Everyone removed himself as far away as possible—except Valentine, who got a pail of water, rushed in, put out the fire, and "saved the battery, but at the risk of his life," an observer recalled.[143]

Another artillery unit that saw much action was the 5th Light Artillery Battery. Before William and James Watterson of Northborough joined it in January of 1864, the 5th had been present at the Second Bull Run, Fredricksburg, Chancellorsville and Gettysburg. Thereafter the pace did not slow; the battery went through the Wilderness-Spotsylvania-Cold Harbor-Weldon Railroad-Petersburg cycle, and finally Appomattox. Its thirty losses were heavy for a company-size unit, but the Wattersons remained sound at the completion of their mission. The ten Northborough men who joined the 4th Heavy Artillery drew less assailable garrison duty near Washington. These gunners did not lose a man to enemy fire, though a few succumbed to disease. All the local men finished their seven-month tour in late 1864 and early 1865 without casualty.

At Andersonville, prisoners are shown burying fellow prisoners. Thirteen thousand men are buried in this graveyard.

Only a few local men rode horses over the battleground. John H. Moore, a thirty-five-year-old carpenter, joined the 1st Regiment Cavalry band on January 6, 1862, but was mustered out in April with a disability. Thomas B. Davis of the same unit was captured and died at Andersonville. Another Northborough member, Dr. Albert Wood, a graduate of Dartmouth College and Harvard Medical School, was appointed a regular army surgeon in

Walter Valentine was a member of the 14th Battery, Light Artillery.

November of 1864 and later became a distinguished civilian practitioner. Captain John C. Wyman served in the 3rd Cavalry Regiment. He also did some staff work for General McClellan, but the high point of his military career came at the end of the war, when he was named a member of the honor guard that accompanied the body of the slain Abraham Lincoln back to Springfield, Illinois.

Much later in life Walter Valentine was a farmer and for two years a Northborough selectman.

CRED

In town everyone knew by late 1864 that the war could not last more than a few months. In the presidential election Lincoln was opposed by General George McClellan, whose disinclination to attack had vexed the president so often in the past. Lincoln's share of the Northborough vote, while smaller

100

A prayer is said over wounded men in Spotsylvania in May of 1864.

than in 1860, was still substantial, 198 to 52.[144] A few days later, General William Tecumseh Sherman, the man usually given credit for the expression "War is Hell," left Atlanta, which he had subdued in June, and began his famous march to the sea. In Richmond, Lee's valiant army was much diminished and its supplies were virtually exhausted. On April 9, 1865, Lee met Grant at Appomattox Courthouse and accepted his terms; officially the war was over.

Most of the regiments could disassemble, and well before the end of the year most of them did. One that did not, the 24th Regiment, which four Northborough men, George W. Allen, William E. Harrington, John W. Lincoln and George Mentzer had joined at its inception in September of 1861, served in six states and saw its share of action, although it did not, as its historian wryly put it, lose enough men for inclusion in military historian William F. Fox's "three hundred fighting regiments." But it was one of the longest-serving units, continuing into 1866. Its mission during these months was primarily the preservation of order and guard duty in Richmond. All the townsmen but Lincoln finished their tours in 1864; he had reenlisted and served until the end: January 20, 1866. The son of Jairus Lincoln, who had spearheaded the campaign against slavery in Northborough, and a sharer of the usual Lincoln family interest in music, John Lincoln held the post of principal musician of the regiment.[145] When the regiment finally came

Above left: Surgeon Albert Wood was promoted from his cavalry regiment to the regular army and practiced medicine notably after the war.

Above right: Captain John C. Wyman served in the 3rd Cavalry Regiment and as a member of the Honor Guard that conducted the body of Abraham Lincoln to Springfield, Illinois.

Left: John Lincoln played the role of band leader in the 24th Massachusetts Infantry Regiment. The son of anti-slavery activist Jairus Lincoln, he remained in the service until 1866.

to Boston in January, Lincoln conducted the band in a concert at Boylston Hall, and then on February 2, five days after their discharge, at another in the Boston Music Hall. A cabinetmaker when he enlisted, Lincoln became a piano maker in Boston after the war.[146]

A look at the Massachusetts census of the year 1865, prepared in August, shows many of the veterans back at their old jobs as farmers, shoemakers and comb makers. One would hardly think that Northborough had changed—unless one noticed the missing names, the names that would appear a few years later on the four sides of the town's monument. How many of the survivors bore physical and psychological ravages of sorts little chronicled then, and only intermittently now?

Epilogue

Post Bellum

Some of the men—Fred Bartlett, George Brigham, Peter Gamache, Guilford Heath and the Mentzers—returned to their farms. Nathaniel Randlett built houses. Albert Wood resigned his position as a United States Army surgeon and became one of the leading medical practitioners in Worcester. Fred Twitchell returned to ornamental comb making and Horace Peverly to painting. Guilford Heath, Josiah Proctor, William S. Harrington, Walter Valentine, Asa Fay Jr. and George Allen all served terms as selectmen. Heath, Randlett and Francis Harrington worked on the committee that built the town's first consolidated elementary school, the Hudson Street School. Others, including two of the most accomplished leaders, Frank T. Leach and Walter Gale, left Northborough.

Among the non-combatants, Lucy Allen, who expressed her astonishment at fugitives like William and Ellen Craft, fell ill and spent the war years in bed, dying in 1866. Her daughter Mary, who hosted many of the abolitionist speakers, lived until 1897. Elizabeth, the most revealing letter writer of the family, became "Miss Lizzie" to practically everyone in town until her death in 1893. Brother William, who had followed abolitionist Wendell Phillips home in 1860 and then taught black children in Arkansas, became a history and classics professor at the University of Wisconsin. He, along with his brother Joseph Henry, who delivered the fiery sermon after the attack on Senator Sumner in the Capitol, and another colleague, composed the Allen and Greenough texts for the study of Latin, editions of which remain in use today. A number of Allen descendents preserved their papers and thus kept their perceptions alive for us.

Columbus Eames, the first Northborough father to lose a son in the war, spent much of his time visiting and assisting other Northborough soldiers.

Asa B. Fay Jr. was a lieutenant in the 34th Massachusetts Infantry Regiment, a postmaster and selectman later in life.

Later he drove the committee that erected the town's monument to its victims and spoke at its dedication on September 17, 1870, a date probably chosen as the eighth anniversary of the Antietam battle, which killed five of the men whom Northborough was honoring. While commending the dead, he saluted the living veterans: "To you, as well as to your fallen comrades,

On this float in Northborough's 1916 celebration are Civil War veterans George Allen, John F. Johnson, Henry Burdett, Hazon Leighton, William Bemis, Cyrus Mentzer, Orin Bailey, Daniel Sawyer, William H. Warren, John Hart, Levi Whitcomb and Guilford Heath. The "Goddess of Liberty" is Heath's daughter, Annie.

we owe all that we possess." Then he turned to the town selectman: "Let me charge you and through your charge the long list of those who shall in after years fill your places to guard well your trust and let no enemy of liberty mar the sacred structure."[147] This charge has been carried out to date; anyone can walk a few steps from the sidewalk on West Main Street and read the names of twenty-nine men who did not return.

Reverend Samuel S. Ashley, another tireless visitor of the combatants, left town to work for the Freedmen's Bureau in the South. Appointed superintendent of education for the southern district of North Carolina after the war, he opened schools for freed blacks. Later he served as president of Straight College for African American students in New Orleans.[148] Back in town in 1880, he administered the federal census in Northborough, counting among its residents a young man who was probably the first educated African American to live in Northborough. Newell Ensley, born in Tennessee in 1852, was studying at Newton Theological Seminary in Newton, Massachusetts. Ensley represented precisely what Ashley had striven to foster. He spoke on "The Colored Man's Claim to an Education" at his graduation and became a college professor.[149]

Reverend Samuel S. Ashley served his congregation in Northborough, the troops whenever he was able and the cause of education in the post-war Reconstruction.

The veterans fell away over a period of decades. The youngest to serve, Walter Mayo, also died young, at age thirty-three in 1879. Josiah Proctor, who established a button factory in Northborough and married Lizzie Burdett, who seems to have been of the same family as Thomas Burdett, who tended him in his initial hospitalization after Ball's Bluff. Josiah and

This monument to Civil War veterans, erected in 1869, was dedicated on September 17, 1870.

Levi Whitcomb, whom Joshua Proctor feared might not survive the war, survived Proctor by a quarter century and wore his uniform at a town celebration in 1916.

Lizzie parented nine children before he succumbed at fifty-one in 1892. Several men lived well into the next century. In 1900, Francis Harrington, president several times at the 57th Infantry Regiment's annual reunions, was named Northborough town clerk, a position he held until his death in 1915. Levi Whitcomb, whose welfare Proctor had worried about in 1862,

The Grand Army of the Republic Hall in Northborough, here decorated for the town's 150th anniversary celebration in 1916, was later destroyed by fire.

appeared in uniform at the town's 150th anniversary celebration a quarter century after Proctor died, passing away himself a few months before the World War I armistice. Asa Fay Jr. managed his aged father's farm for a number of years and served as town postmaster under Presidents Harrison, McKinley and Theodore Roosevelt, dying in 1919 at age eighty; Walter Valentine, cool disposer of an explosive at the Weldon Railroad, also died at eighty a year later.

The next casualty was not a man but the Grand Army of the Republic Hall, which stood on Main Street shortly east of the town center until it burned in 1922. The Northborough G.A.R. post bore the name of Sergeant Joseph N. Johnson, an Antietam victim. The last Civil War veteran to die locally was Harrington's Company K buddy in the 57th Infantry, Guilford P. Heath, at age eighty-eight in 1931, nearly seventy years after the first shots of the war and thirteen years after the World War, when some observers were beginning to fear that world wars might have to be numbered.

Despite the immensity of world wars, about as many American soldiers died in the Civil War as in the two world wars combined, when the population was several times higher. Deaths from disease and from wounds far outran those of later wars. The word "disability" is all one can easily learn about what happened to many injured veterans in the 1860s, and that term was normally applied only to physical impairments. Heroes are usually tight-lipped; others do not know—perhaps do not even want to guess—what nightmares these veterans encountered.

But old soldiers have memories also and take pride in having done what they were asked to do. Looking back, one can argue that the Civil War, in its long, bloody, lamentable way, helped make possible *a more perfect union.*

Appendix

Men Who Served in the Civil War

T here are three lists below. The account in Josiah C. Kent's *Northborough History*, which William H. Mulligan Jr. repeated in *Northborough: A Town and Its People, 1638–1975*, includes the first two lists but regards all of the men as Northborough men, although some in the second list, while credited to the Northborough quota, never lived in Northborough. The third list, which includes people with Northborough connections after the war, are omitted in Kent and Mulligan, although some of the men became Northborough fixtures. I cannot guarantee that the list is complete, but it is more complete and less misleading than the lists included in the two histories mentioned above.

1. Civil War veterans who lived in Northborough at the time of their enlistment

Allen, George W.	Farwell, Charles B.	Mayo, Charles L.
Arlen, Doctor	Fay, Asa B., Jr.	Mentzer, Cyrus
Ashton, Thomas	Fay, Leander	Mentzer, George
Austin, Caleb S.	Felton, Charles A.	Merriam, George F.
Babcock, William B.	Fiske, George W.	Minot, Justin
Ball, Lucius	Fitzpatrick, John	Montague, Daniel
Bartlett, Frederick	Fletcher, Lorenzo	Moore, John H.
Bemis, Adelbert W.	Fuller, Nathaniel	Peverly, Horace L.
Billings, Charles E.	Gale, Walter	Proctor, Joseph H.
Bonner, James F.	Gamache, Peter	Proctor, Josiah
Breach, Thomas	Gates, George H.	Prouty, George S.
Brewer, Henry C.	Glazier, Asaph	Randlett, Nathaniel

Brine, John A.

Bucklin, Alonzo K.

Burdett, Jerome W.

Burke, John

Carcagne, Frank

Carruth, Albert H.

Carruth, Joseph W.

Chapin, George P.

Cheever, George H.

Clemence, William L.

Coleman, Darius

Conant, Leonard W.

Cutler, Silas A.

Dandurand, Austin

Davis, James

Davis, Joseph A.

Day, Henry J.

Dudley, Joseph

Dunn, Michael

Eames, Warren F.

Fairbanks, Alonzo P.

Fairbanks, Joseph J.

Gleason, Spencer W.

Goulding, Henry C.

Hanley, Francis

Heath, Guilford P.

Hodgkins, Nathaniel

Hodgkins, Samuel

Johnson, James N.

Johnson, John F.

Johnson, Joseph P.

Johnson, Lewis

Johnson, Willam H.

Kaighn, Charles T.

Kingman, Lucius

Kinney, Henry

Larkin, John P.

Leach, Frank T.

Lewis, Charles H.

Lincoln, John W.

Lowell, Edward

Mahan, Thomas

Maynard, Waldo B.

Rich, William A.

Richardson, Edward P.

Richardson, Gustavus

Sanford, William F.

Sargent, Henry

Seymour, Lewis

Shaw, Charles L.

Smith, Charles E.

Stacy, Albert H.

Stone, James L.

Stone, Lyman

Towle, Perry W.

Trowbridge, Charles A.

Twitchell, Frederick L.

Warren, Charles E.

Watterson, James

Watterson, William

Woodward, Thomas N., Jr.

Yeaw, Daniel

Yeaw, Jesse L.

Yeaw, Welcome P.

2. Men enrolled from Northborough but not Northborough residents at the time. (Where known, the residence is given after the name. Many of the following men had Northborough connections such as birth or extensive prior residence there.)

Aldrich, William M. (Westborough)

Bacon, Charles W. (Westborough)

Bailey, S. Henry (Worcester)

Baird, James Herbert (Marlborough)

Ball, David H. (Worcester)

Beaman, William (Winchendon)

Bemis, Ezra (Southborough)

Bonner, George C. (not listed)

Bonner, William (not listed)

Bowers, Francis A. (Clinton)

Breach, John (not listed)

Brigham, George C. (Marlborough)

Brigham, James H. (not listed)

Burdett, Thomas E. (Lancaster)

Knight, George W. (Milford)

Miles, Samuel J. (Marlborough)

Muzzy, Charles C. (Worcester)

Nelson, John (Worcester)

Nolan, Daniel (not listed)

Norcross, Thomas A. (Sutton)

Overton, Richard (not listed)

Palmer, John T. (not listed)

Pierce, Edwin W. (Worcester)

Rice, Moses P. (Marlborough)

Rice, Walter C. (Lancaster)

Robbins, Arthur W. (Westborough)

Russell, Henry (not listed)

Smith, Alfred (Thompson, Conn.)

Men Who Served in the Civil War

Carter, Charles W. (Clinton)
Cashen, John (not listed)
Clemons, Walter (Westborough)
Craig, John W. (Stoneham)
Cunningham, John (Roxbury)
Davis, Thomas B. (Lawrence)
Duffee, John R. (Salem)
Forbes, John M. (Boylston)
Glazier, Joseph S. (Cambridgeport)
Green, Allen (Boston)
Green, Lorenzo B. (West Boylston)
Harrington, William E. (Westborough)
Holman, Henry B. (Clinton)
Kirby, Thomas (Boston)

Stearns, John M. (Douglas)
Steen, John (not listed)
Sullivan, James H. (Westborough)
Taylor, Robert (not listed)
Valentine, Walter (Boston)
Warren, William H. (North Brookfield)
Wetherbee, Emory (Marlborough)
Whitcomb, Levi (New Bedford)
Williams, Warren (Southborough)
Wood, Albert (not listed)
Wood, Henry F. (Marlborough)
Wyman, Benjamin F. (Lancaster)
Wyman, John C. (Boston)

3. Men not listed above, but for whom Northborough Veterans' Graves Registrations or other proofs of residence exist. (For the most part these are men who settled in Northborough at some time after the war. Some of the men are not buried in Northborough. This list also includes the names of the only five known men with Northborough connections who served in the United States Navy.)

Ball, Lyman E.
Baird, William P. (Navy)
Bailey, David Mince
Brigham, Charles L. (Army, Navy)
Brooks, Helon
Burdett, Henry Helon
Clark, James M. (Navy)
Cole, Ebenezer
Corey, Theodore F.
Cotting, Edward P.
Cummings, Joseph Howard
Eager, John W.
Falby, Andrew W.J. (Navy)
Fay, Hiram
Gage, Samuel C.
Glazier, Henry
Harrington, Francis Moore

Harris, William Bradford
Hart, John F.
Haven, Charles W.
Howe, Steven A.
Johnson, Luther
Johnston, William
Leighton, Hazon
Lewis, John A.
Love, Charles T.
Lucius, Charles E.
Lynch, John T.
McKenzie, David Banks (Navy)
Mentzer, Charles L.
Mills, Samuel F.
Mitchell, Edwin Andrew
Murray, George H.
Newton, Charles M.
Parker, Edward S.

Parmenter, Henry L.
Parmenter, John Wesley
Robinson, Orry Mandel
Sargent, Pliney
Sawyer, Daniel R.
Smith, Charles Edwin
Smith, Francis Lyman
Spencer, George W.
Staples, Augustus Milton
Stone, William E.
Stratton, Edward B.
Thompson, Mial M.
Whitney, Leonard M.
Whittemore, Joseph
Wills, George
Wilson, Oliver
Wood, Edward W.

Notes

Prologue

1. Federal census of Northborough, 1860, prepared about nine months before the commencement of the Civil War.

2. Josiah Coleman Kent, *Northborough History* (Newton, MA: Garden City Press, 1921), p. 193.

3. Kent, p. 14. The reference to the Peverley marriage and the son is based on the present author's unpublished *Northborough Vital Records 1851–1892*, derived from vital records in the office of the Northborough town clerk.

4. *Aegis & Transcript*, Worcester, MA, November 10, 1860.

5. American Antiquarian Society (hereafter "AAS"), *Allen-Johnson Family Papers*, Box 3, Folder 34.

6. *Allen-Johnson Family Papers*, Box 3, Folder 34.

7. *Allen-Johnson Family Papers*, Box 1, Folder 9.

Chapter 1

8. Northborough Historical Society (hereafter "NHS") 2006.4.3.B.27, Lucy Clark Allen to Catherine Thaxter, March 9, 1828.

9. Carl Bode, *The American Lyceum: Town Meeting of the Mind* (Carbondale: Southern Illinois University Press, 1968) is a good introduction to this subject.

10. There is no image available of this building, which burned in 1870. Harriet H. Johnson, the granddaughter of Dr. Allen, described it in a talk given at the Northborough Historical Society in 1912. NHS Folder 22.A.4.

11. NHS 12.1. *The Meteor*, November 19, 1836. This newspaper is another manifestation of Allen family influence. Joseph and Lucy maintained a boarding school and the newspaper was published and printed by its students.

12. Henry Mayer, *All on Fire: William Lloyd Garrison and the Abolition of Slavery* (New York: St. Martin's Griffin, 1998), p. 120.

13. *Allen-Johnson Family Papers*, Octavo Volume 20.

14. NHS 12.1. The February 18 and March 18 issues of *The Meteor* refer to the discussion continued from February 15 to February 22.

15. NHS 68.48.38, the journal of Samuel Fisher, November 2, 1837 entry.

16. Mary Fuhrer, a student of Mary White's activities, in an e-mail message to the author on September 8, 2006, alleged that she had found no evidence of Mary White ever speaking in public. "I wish I could confirm that this remarkable entry refers to Mary White, but unfortunately I cannot," she wrote. However, the only alternatives seem to be the existence of two Mary Whites with pronounced anti-slavery views in the small village of Boylston, or some sort of error on the part of Fisher in reporting the event.

17. NHS 68.48.38, Samuel Fisher's journal, December 5, 1837.

18. Ibid., Fisher's journal, December 19, 1837.

19. Ibid., 68.48.38, Fisher's journal, February 11, 1838.

20. Ibid., Fisher's journal, March 28, 1839.

Chapter 2

21. William H. Mulligan Jr., *Northborough: A Town and Its People, 1638–1975* (Northborough, MA: Northborough American Revolution Bicentennial Commission, 1981), p. 270.

22. John W. Blassingame, ed., *The Frederick Douglass Papers, Series One: Speeches, Debates, and Interviews, Vol. I, 1841–1846* (New Haven: Yale University Press, 1979), pp. lxxxviii and vi.

23. Deborah E. McDowell, ed., *Narrative of the Life of Frederick Douglass: An American Slave* (New York: Oxford University Press, 1999), p. 88. Douglass's assertion appears early in chapter 11 of his narrative.

24. NHS Folder 2A.4.

25. Ibid. Joseph Henry Allen's letter is written on the document he received from the Anti-Slavery Society.

26. NHS 2001.8.16. Reverend Allen's essay is written in a composition notebook and was apparently not intended for public consumption.

27. This attribution is included in a newspaper obituary of Jairus Lincoln pasted into Lincoln's copy of B. Porteus, *Lectures on the Gospel of St. Matthew, NHS 73.79.1.*

28. Robin W. Winks, ed., *Four Fugitive Slave Narratives* (Reading, MA: Addison-Wesley Publishing Company, 1969), pp. 81–82. The four sections of this book are paged separately; the references here and hereafter are to the second section of the book.

29. Winks, p. 88.

30. Ibid., p. 92.

31. Ibid., p. 98.

32. NHS 2006.4.8.11.

33. NHS Folder 24.B.24.

34. NHS 2006.4.1.C.18.

35. *National Aegis* (Worcester, MA), November 22, 1848.

36. NHS 2006.4.1.C.21.

37. NHS 2006.4.1.C.23.

38. NHS Folder 22.A.5.

39. NHS 2006.4.2.C.20.

40. NHS Folder 22.A.4.

41. NHS 2006.4.1.C.24.

42. Kathryn Grover, a well-known scholar of the Underground Railroad, wrote to me asking about Cook. She included the following quotation from the *Leominster* [Massachusetts] *Daily Enterprise* of March 25, 1910: "Calvin B. Cook…was one of the famous underground men and made many trips from Northboro, where he lived, to Leominster, with two or three refugees at a time and would hand them over to some of the men who lived here." I responded: "Calvin B. Cook appears in the Northborough assessors' records throughout the 1840s and in the 1850 census. From these documents it appears that he was a comb maker (a common occupation in Northborough at the time), as were at least three of his sons. His wife was named Miriam. He does not appear to have owned any real property. His name shows up as one of the signers of a petition signed by 172 Northborough men, probably during June of 1848, recommending what actually did come about that year: presidential and vice-presidential candidates opposed to the extension of slavery. Just how long he remained in Northborough I cannot say, our records for the 1850's being sparse, but his name does not appear in the Massachusetts state census of Northborough for 1855. His son Charles remained for some time thereafter in town."

43. The program of the play is NHS Folder 22.B.29.

44. NHS 2001.8.37.

Chapter 3

45. AAS, Allen-Johnson Family Papers, Box 1, Folder 10.

46. *Massachusetts Soldiers, Sailors, and Marines in the Civil War,* (Norwood, MA: Norwood Press, 1931), I.95, V. 561, V.158. This work is indexed and information easy to locate; specific volume and page references will not be included hereafter.

47. Kent, pp. 225–233.

48. NHS Folder 50.1 and 50.4.

49. NHS 69.14.13. Columbus Eames's diary will be cited by date of entry.

50. Kent, p. 216.

51. NHS Folder 24.B.22.C.

52. Kent, p. 217.

53. NHS Folder 24.B.22.C, October 25, 1861.

54. Ted Ballard, *Battle of Ball's Bluff* (Washington: Center of Military History, United States Army, 2001), p. 37.

55. Mulligan, pp. 128–129.

56. NHS 63.51.2. A set of Josiah Proctor's letters home was later typed and donated to the Northborough Historical Society by his son Edwin.

57. Kent, p. 218.

58. Ibid., p. 218.

59. NHS 2006.4.1.L.59.

60. Richard F. Miller, *Harvard's Civil War: A History of the Twentieth Massachusetts Volunteer Infantry* (Hanover, NH: University Press of New England, 2005), pp. 86–87. Woodward was a member of the Massachusetts 15th, but prisoners of several military units were all subjected to the treatment which Miller describes.

61. Mulligan, pp.146–147.

62. Kent, pp. 225–232.

Chapter 4

63. NHS Folder 24.B.4.

64. Miller, p. 118.

65. Kent, p. 232.

66. NHS 63.5.2, letter 8.

67. NHS 63.5.2, letter 9.

68. Kent, p. 232.

69. E-mail message to this author from Linda Green, Acton [Massachusetts] Historical Society, November 19, 2006.

70. Kent, pp. 225–232.

71. NHS 2006.4.1.C.65.

72. NHS 2006.4.1.H.34.

73. NHS 2006.4.1.H.35.

74. Kent, p. 232.

75. Stephen W. Sears, *Landscape Turned Red: The Battle of Antietam* (New Haven: Ticknor & Fields, 1983), pp. 227–228.

76. NHS 2006.4.1.L.64; website www.nextech.de/ma15mvi.

77. This letter is quoted on the website indicated above, a large portion of which is devoted to "Roster and Genealogies of the 15th Massachusetts Volunteer Infantry: 1861–1864."

78. NHS 2006.4.1.L.67.

79. James M. McPherson, *Crossroads of Freedom: Antietam* (New York: Oxford University Press, 2002), p. xvi.

80. NHS 24.B.9.

81. NHS 63.51.2, letter 12.

82. Ibid., letter 13.

83. Ibid., letter 14.

84. Ibid., letter 18.

85. Ibid., letter 19.

86. NHS 2004.4.1.L.73.

87. Gale died in Santa Barbara, California, according to website www.nextech.de/ma15mvi.

Chapter 5

88. NHS 2006.4.1.L.75.

89. NHS 2006.4.1.L.76.

90. On the work of the Sanitary Commission, an excellent source of information is Mary Ashton Rice Livermore, *My Story of the War: A Woman's Narrative of Four Years Personal Experience*...(New York: De Capo Press, 1995), a reprint of the original edition of 1887.

91. NHS 2006.1.L.85.

92. Alfred S. Roe, *The Twenty-Fourth Regiment Massachusetts Volunteers 1861–1866* (Worcester: Twenty-Fourth Veteran Association, 1907), pp. 215–226.

93. 2006.4.1.L.92.

94. NHS 2006.4.1.L.93. There is also information on William Allen's work at two educational web sites, www.library.wisc.edu at the University of Wisconsin, where he taught for many years and at http://docsouth.unc.edu at the University of North Carolina. In NHS 62.1.140.B.1, the diary of Ellen Crosby, the diarist records on February 7 an account of William Allen's visit to a Northborough school where she taught. He gave an account of his Arkansas teaching experience to the children.

95. *Town of Northborough Annual Report, 1862-1863*, pp. 8–11.

96. NHS 2005.5.1.

97. William S. Lincoln, *Life with the Thirty-Fourth Mass. Infantry in the War of the Rebellion* (Worcester: Noyes, Snow & Company, 1879), p. 59.

98. Kent, p. 232.

99. NHS Folder 24.B.23.C. This is a manuscript by Edwin A. Wood, "A Brief History, Company A, 51st Regiment Volunteers," undated, p. 7.

100. Kent, pp. 225–232 and Northborough vital records maintained by the town clerk.

101. Wood, p. 7.

102. NHS 24.B.30.

103. Kent, p. 232.

104. www.nextech.de/ma15mvi.

105. NHS 63.51.2, Letter 35.

106. NHS 63.51.2, unnumbered letter dated February 5, 1864.

107. NHS 97.32.5.A.

108. Clark, p. 66.

109. Kent, pp. 232–233.

110. J. Waldo Denny, *Wearing the Blue in the Twenty-Fifth Mass. Volunteer Infantry with Burnside's Coast Division, 18th Army Corps, Army of the James* (Worcester: Putnam & Davis, 1879), p. 336.

111. Clark, p. 68.

112. John Anderson, *The Fifty-Seventh Regiment of Massachusetts Volunteers in the War of the Rebellion* (Boston: E. B. Stillings & Co., 1896), p. 4.

113. NHS C.19.1, 53rd Regiment diary of Francis M. Harrington.

114. NHS C.19.2, 57th Regiment diary of Francis M. Harrington. This work will be cited by dates given in text.

115. Anderson, p. 24.

116. Ibid., p. 37.

117. Ibid., p. 40.

118. Ibid., p. 68.

119. Ibid., p. 72.

Chapter 6

120. Anderson, p. 130.

121. Ibid., p. 131.

122. NHS 57.1.26.B.

123. Anderson, p. 140.

124. Ibid., p. 173.

125. Ibid., p. 160.

126. Ibid., p. 176.

127. Ibid., p. 177.

128. Ibid., p. 179.

129. Ibid., p. 180.

130. Ibid., pp. 185–186.

131. Clark, p. 82.

132. Anderson, p. 186.

133. Ibid., pp. 191–192.

134. Kent, pp. 232–233.

135. Lincoln, pp. 126, 192, 250.

136. Ibid., p. 385.

137. Ibid., pp. 390-391.

138. Ibid., p. 408; Kent, p. 229.

139. Edward F. Roberts, *Andersonville Journey* (Shippensburg, PA: Burd Street Press, 1998), p. 88.

140. Kent, p. 232.

141. Roberts, p. xi–xii.

142. Kent, p. 233; Roberts, p. 84.

143. NHS, Folder 24.B.10.

144. *Aegis & Transcript* (Worcester), November 12, 1864.

145. Roe, p. 483.

146. Ibid., pp. 441–442.

Epilogue

147. NHS 71.53.6

148. John L. Bell, "Samuel Stanford Ashley, Carpetbagger and Educator," *The North Carolina Historical Review* 72 (1995): 456–483, *passim*.

149. Archives and Special Collections, Trask Library, Andover Newton Theological School, Newton Centre, Massachusetts.

Bibliography

PUBLISHED WORKS

Anderson, John. *The Fifty-Seventh Regiment of Massachusetts Volunteers in the War of the Rebellion.* Boston: E.B. Stillings, 1896.

Ayers, Edward L. *In the Presence of Mine Enemies: War in the Heart of America, 1859–1863.* New York: W.W. Norton & Company, 2003.

Ballard, Ted. *Battle of Ball's Bluff. Washington: Center of Military History*, United States Army, 2001.

Bell, John L. "Samuel Stanford Ashley, Carpetbagger and Educator." *The North Carolina Historical Review*, vol. lxxii, no. 4 (October 1995): 456–483

Blackett, R.J.M., ed. *Running a Thousand Miles for Freedom: The Escape of William and Ellen Craft from Slavery.* Baton Rouge: Louisiana State University Press, 1999.

Blassingame, John W., ed. *The Frederick Douglass Papers, Series One: Speeches, Debates, and Interviews, 1841–1846.* New Haven: Yale University Press, 1979.

Bode, Carl. *The American Lyceum: Town Meeting of the Mind.* Carbondale: Southern Illinois University Press, 1968.

Bruce, George A. *The Twentieth Regiment of Massachusetts Volunteer Infantry, 1861–1865.* Boston: Houghton, Mifflin and Company, 1906.

Clark, Henry. *My Experience with Burnside's Expedition and 18ᵗʰ Army Corps*. Gardner, MA, 1914.

Denny, J. Waldo. *Wearing the Blue in the Twenty-Fifth Mass. Volunteer Infantry with Burnside's Coast Division, 18ᵗʰ Army Corps, Army of the James*. Worcester, MA: Putnam & Davis, 1879.

Ease, David M. *History of the Excursion of the Fifteenth Massachusetts Regiment*. Worcester, MA, 1886.

Four Fugitive Slave Narratives. Reading, MA: Addison-Wesley Publishing Co., 1969.

Furgurson, Ernest B. *Not War but Murder: Cold Harbor, 1864*. New York: Alfred A. Knopf, 2000.

Kent, Josiah Coleman. *Northborough History*. Newton, MA: Garden City Press, Inc., 1921.

Lincoln, William S. *Life with the Thirty-Fourth Mass. Infantry in the War of the Rebellion*. Worcester, MA: Noyes, Snow & Company, 1879.

Livermore, Mary Ashton Rice. *My Story of the War: A Woman's Narrative of Four Years Personal Experience*. New York: Da Capo Press, 1995.

Massachusetts Soldiers, Sailors, and Marines in the Civil War. 8 vols. Norwood, MA: Norwood Press, 1931.

Mayer, Henry. *All on Fire: William Lloyd Garrison and the Abolition of Slavery*. New York: St. Martin's Griffin, 1998.

Mayfield, John. *Rehearsal for Republicanism: Free Soil and the Politics of Antislavery*. Port Washington, NY: Kennikat Press, 1980.

McDowell, Deborah E., ed. *Narrative of the Life of Frederick Douglass: An American Slave*. New York: Oxford University Press, 1999.

McPherson, James M. *Crossroads of Freedom: Antietam*. New York: Oxford University Press, 2002.

Miller, Richard F. *Harvard's Civil War: A History of the Twentieth Massachusetts Volunteer Infantry*. Hanover, NH: University Press of New England, 2005.

Mulligan, William H., Jr. *Northborough: A Town and Its People, 1638–1975*. Northborough, MA: Northborough American Revolution Bicentennial Commission, 1981.

Nutt, Charles. *History of Worcester and Its People*. 4 vols. New York: Lewis Historical Publishing Company, 1919.

Rayback, Joseph G. *Free Soil: The Election of 1848*. Lexington: University of Kentucky Press, 1970.

Rhea, Gordon C. *The Battle of the Wilderness: May 5–6, 1864*. Baton Rouge: Louisiana State University Press, 1994.

Roberts, Edward F. *Andersonville Journey*. Shippensburg, PA: Burd Street Press, 1998.

Roe, Alfred S. *The Twenty-Fourth Regiment: Massachusetts Volunteers, 1861–1866*. Worcester, MA: Twenty-Fourth Veteran Association, 1907.

Schouler, William. *History of Massachusetts in the Civil War*. 2 vols. Boston: E.P. Dutton & Company, 1871.

Sears, Stephen W. *Landscape Turned Red: The Battle of Antietam*. New Haven: Ticknor & Fields, 1983.

Stout, Harry S. *Upon the Altar of the Nation: A Moral History of the American Civil War*. New York: Viking, 2006.

Town of Northborough Annual Report, 1862–1863. Northborough, MA, 1863.

Winks, Robin W., ed. *Four Fugitive Slave Narratives*. Reading, MA: Addison-Wesley Publishing Company, 1969.

Unpublished Works

American Antiquarian Society, Worcester, MA. Allen-Johnson Family Papers.

Northborough Historical Society. Archival collection.

Wood, Edwin A. "A Brief History, Company A, 51st Regiment Volunteers," undated.

BIBLIOGRAPHY

Newspapers

Aegis & Transcript, Worcester, MA, November 10, 1860.

Daily Enterprise. Leominister, MA, March 25, 1910.

Meteor, Northborough, MA, November 19, 1836; February 18 and March 18, 1837.

National Aegis, Worcester, MA, November 22, 1848.

Web Sites

Harnwell, Colin D. and Edward B. Ralph. Site contains "Roster and Genealogies of the 15th Massachusetts Volunteer Infantry," 1861–1864. http://www.nextech.de/ma15mvi

University of Wisconsin. http://www.library.wisc.edu

University of North Carolina. http://docsouth.unc.edu

Please visit us at

www.historypress.net